ITA WEGMAN, MD (1876–1943) was co-responsible for founding Anthroposophical Medicine alongside Rudolf Steiner. Born in the Dutch East Indies, she trained in gymnastics and massage and later medicine. She founded the first anthroposophical medical clinic (now the Ita Wegman Clinic), created a gentle form of massage therapy (Rhythmical Massage), and developed a cancer treatment following indications from Steiner based on mistletoe (Iscador). She also founded a therapeutic home for mentally handicapped children (Haus Sonnenhof) and co-founded a pharmaceutical laboratory (Weleda), that is now a major producer of medicines and healthcare products. In 1923 Ita Wegman joined the Executive Council of the newly reformed Anthroposophical Society at the Goetheanum in Dornach, Switzerland, where she directed the Medical Section. Wegman and Steiner co-authored *Extending Practical Medicine*, which gives an introduction and theoretical basis to Anthroposophical Medicine.

D1254027

ITA WEGMAN
Esoteric Studies

The Michael Impulse

TEMPLE LODGE

Compiled and translated by Crispian Villeneuve

Temple Lodge Publishing
Hillside House, The Square
Forest Row, RH18 5ES

www.templelodge.com

First published by Temple Lodge 1993
Reprinted 2013

Originally published in English as articles (see details in Foreword, pp. 12–14)

This translation and compilation © Temple Lodge Publishing 1993

A catalogue record for this book is available from the British Library

ISBN 978 1 906999 47 6

Cover by Morgan Creative featuring photo of Ita Wegman by kind permission of the Ita Wegman Institute, Arlesheim (special thanks to Peter Selg and Thomas O'Keefe)
Typeset by DP Photosetting, Neath, West Glamorgan
Printed and bound by Berforts Ltd., Herts.

Contents

Foreword

This volume is being published to mark the fiftieth anniversary in 1993 of the death of Ita Wegman, and to launch a new series on the pioneers of modern spiritual science from Temple Lodge Publishing.

To an English readership Ita Wegman is still largely known as the doctor who collaborated with Rudolf Steiner in the writing of a medical textbook. This book appeared with the somewhat elaborate German title *Grundlegendes für eine Erweiterung der Heilkunst nach geisteswissenschaftlichen Erkenntnissen.* At Rudolf Steiner's express request to D.N. Dunlop in 1924, it was also brought out in an English edition, translated by George Adams; this latter carries the simpler title *Fundamentals of Therapy.* Like its German original, the English translation first appeared in late 1925, several months after Rudolf Steiner's death. It has been reprinted on and off ever since.

Anybody reasonably well acquainted with Rudolf Steiner's literary works will also be aware that the writing of this book was the only occasion when he collaborated in a joint production. In this sense alone—dual authorship—it stands somewhat apart from all his other writings, to which, however, it is also intimately connected by explicit reference in its very first chapter. An interested reader can follow up these connections by consulting this or that publication cited therein, and so bring this book, too, into suitable contextual relation with Rudolf Steiner's works—and thereby also his person—as a whole.

With regard to Ita Wegman's part in the book, however, such a contextual relation has for its English readership been hitherto largely precluded by reason of the fact that other writings by her have not been made so generally available. So this one work which she wrote in collaboration with Rudolf

Steiner has been left to stand in its reader's consciousness in a somewhat peculiar and perhaps even intriguing position. In its own field it is clearly a work of importance, but does it actually present the main part of Wegman's literary legacy? Since Rudolf Steiner explicitly declared in London in 1924 that Ita Wegman was his 'dear friend and co-worker in medical and other fields of spiritual research, in the whole field of spiritual research' one may well wonder why the part of such research made most generally available in the English language should be that which is restricted to the medical field.

The answer to this question must itself be put in perspective by stating at the outset that Ita Wegman was not anyway primarily an author. She never on her own wrote any complete book as such. In this respect, too, it may well be relevant that Rudolf Steiner himself also remarked of her: 'Frau Wegman is a woman of deeds, not of words.'

And yet that very remark will doubtless also remind the reader of a famous passage in Part 1 of Goethe's *Faust*: the protagonist is found engaged in translating the opening sentence of St John's Gospel, and after considering various alternatives for 'In the beginning was the Word' Faust finally decides on the version 'In the beginning was the Deed'. Goethe divined here that the context at issue brings these two concepts into identity. The whole point about the incarnation of that Word on Earth was precisely that His deeds were utterly matched to His words.

That Ita Wegman has recently been found deserving of a biographical documentation running to no fewer than three volumes should suffice to indicate that her life was remarkable. And the deeds of which that life consisted were inextricably intertwined with what she said and what she also wrote. For although authorship was not in itself her main occupation she certainly made a very powerful, indeed at times positively searing impact on the consciousness of her contemporaries by the medium of the written word.

Apart from the medical textbook produced jointly with Rudolf Steiner, Ita Wegman's excursions into the literary domain took two forms. One of these was the compilation

of the book *Aus Michaels Wirken*, which first appeared in
1929. This is a collection of legends from many lands and
cultures about the Archangel Michael, deliberately aimed at a
popular readership but nonetheless produced with the highest
devotion and most scrupulous care. It was introduced by her
and given an extensive essay from her hand comprising her
finest and most sustained piece of writing on the work of this
Archangel in the course of human history. The book has been
many times reprinted and is still today as readable and
spiritually inspiring as when it first appeared.

The other form of written expression was that of articles, of
which a steady flow came from her pen over the years 1925 to
1932. That these were by no means so ephemeral as to be
easily consigned to oblivion is shown by the fact that some
years after her death two separate collections of them were
made, the first with a characteristically long German title, and
the second with a short and markedly curious one. *In Anbruch
des Wirkens für eine Erweiterung der Heilkunst nach geistes-
wissenschaftlicher Menschenkunde* was published in 1956. It
contains all the articles which she wrote for the medical
monthly *Natura* (over the years 1926 to 1932). *An die Freunde*
was published in 1960. It contains a large selection of her
articles (supposedly the 'essential' ones, though essential to
what is nowhere explained) from the weekly anthroposophical
newsheet *Was in der Anthroposophischen Gesellschaft vorgeht*
from the years 1925 to 1927. The reader of this latter selection
is not informed that from various of these articles certain
passages have been excised.

Both of these volumes have subsequently gone into further
impressions. But neither of them have found any mirroring in
the English language. And although this state of affairs might
not otherwise be regarded as anything very unusual what
makes it particularly thought-provoking in the case of Ita
Wegman is the fact that it was precisely into an English-
reading context that a large part of her energies came to be
channelled. The present volume provides ample testimony of
this. With regard to her own writings, the translation of the
book that came out as *Fundamentals of Therapy* was produced
with striking rapidity, and every single article which she wrote

for the Dornach anthroposophical news-sheet over the years 1925 to 1927 appeared also in English translation in the weekly *Anthroposophical Movement* in issues published on the very same day on which the issues containing their German originals came out on the Continent. This fact alone suffices to show the importance which was attached to intimacy and speed of collaboration between Dornach and London in those early anthroposophical years. In an article 'The English Edition of the *Weekly News*' appearing in the 11 March 1928 issue, George Adams (Kaufmann) spent some paragraphs reminiscing about this earlier period and the relation of the English news-sheet to the German-language one published in Dornach: 'The Weekly News of the General Anthroposophical Society was begun ... in January 1924, immediately after the Christmas Foundation Meeting ... In England, to begin with, we printed a monthly abridged edition, containing only Dr Steiner's contributions and the more important announcements from Dornach. Dr Steiner, however, was not satisfied with this; he was anxious for the whole English-speaking world to share in what is going on in Dornach and elsewhere, equally with those who are able to read the original ... The *Vorstand* asked us in London to undertake the issue of an edition for the English-speaking world as a whole. This was a call to which we felt we must respond ... and in the early summer of 1924 we published the first number of the *Weekly News* in English ... Our task was to translate the Dornach edition as quickly as possible and circulate it week by week to the subscribers in Great Britain, America, Australia, New Zealand and so on ... The immediate translation of about 5,000 words weekly is no easy matter. From the beginning, a number of members gave us their loyal and constant co-operation in this work. Mr Collison was editor of the English edition and I acted as his assistant ...' In this way the English reader of the time came to have as much and as immediate access to the articles which Ita Wegman was supplying for the German-language news-sheet as did his German-reading contemporary. From 1926 onwards several of the longer articles that Wegman was writing for *Natura* also began to appear in English in the quarterly *Anthroposophy*, though here with a definite time-lag after the appearance of the originals. The main purpose of the present volume is to allow the English reader of today to share in these reading experiences of his anthroposophical predecessors of the late 1920s, and then to listen to Wegman's own spoken voice from the early 1930s.

* * *

For a real appreciation of Ita Wegman's life the reader is referred to the previously mentioned documentary trilogy by J.E. Zeylmans van Emmichoven, *Wer war Ita Wegman?* (1990–92). In the context of the present Foreword only a brief account can be given, and for reasons implicit in the previous section this account takes particular note of the texts which are here reproduced and their consequences.

Ita Wegman was born on 22 February 1876 in a house on a sugar plantation at Parakanteroes, near Karavang, some 40 miles east of present-day Jakarta, in Java. Her father had emigrated from Holland to the then Dutch East Indies at an early age, entered the sugar trade and quickly risen to become manager of the Parakanteroes sugar-factory. He had married a Dutch girl, Henriette Offers, in 1875 and Maria Hendrika, always called 'Ita', was their first child, with four more children following. When Ita reached the age of 6 the family moved some three hundred miles further east, near the town of Probolinggo on the Javan north coast, dominated by a mountain range including three towering volcanoes and the gigantic Mount Semeru. Here in Probolinggo Ita went to school till about the age of 12, after which she also had some private tuition.

Her youngest brother, Henry-Charles, died, probably from cholera, in the year 1890, and it may have been as a result of this blow that the parents decided to send their two elder children to finish their education in Europe. Accompanied by their mother, Ita (now aged about 14) and her sister Charlien made the long sea journey from Java all the way to Holland. For about the next four years the two girls lived in Arnheim and went to school in that town, eagerly absorbing the to them wholly new European cultural ambience, and during school holidays visiting other European countries as well. In 1895 they then returned to Java, Ita being now 19 years old. On this return journey she made the acquaintance of a young officer, to whom she soon became engaged. But he died shortly afterwards from tuberculosis.

Ita then retreated for a few years to a house which her father owned in the mountains, immersing herself in the theosophical literature with which she had already become acquainted. After the whole new world which she had discovered in Holland she now anyway came to find life in the colonial circles of Dutch Indonesia somewhat tedious by comparison. When therefore in the year 1900 her parents happened to be travelling on their own account to Holland it was agreed that Ita—by this time aged 25—should accompany them and be allowed to pursue in Europe her now intended career of therapeutic gymnast and masseuse.

So once more she returned to Holland, and this time stayed in Europe for good. For the next two years she lived in Haarlem, doing a training in gymnastics and gaining a suitable diploma. She then travelled to Berlin, where after a study of Swedish massage she began to work in a therapeutic institute. During all this time she had also kept up her theosophical interests, and so when she arrived in Berlin in the late summer of 1902 she also came to meet the man who was about to take over as General Secretary of the German Section of the Theosophical Society, Dr Rudolf Steiner.

Although Ita Wegman duly became a member of this German Section, a real interest in what Rudolf Steiner was conveying in his lectures did not awaken in her until April 1904, when she heard him lecturing on Goethe's *Fairy Tale*. She attended the Theosophical Congress in Amsterdam in that summer, and early in the following year, 1905, she had a conversation with Rudolf Steiner in which the latter advised her to give up Swedish massage and curative gymnastics and take up instead the study of medicine. Since at that time there was no possibility for a woman to take up such a study at a German university, Rudolf Steiner pointed her towards Switzerland.

Ita Wegman accordingly moved to Zurich, and in the event

stayed there for the next 15 years. After a general academic preparation she matriculated at Zurich University in 1906, and then began—at the age of 30—to immerse herself in the lengthy process of a medical training. In this she was periodically encouraged by Rudolf Steiner during his occasional Zurich visits, and she in turn also continued to participate in the progress of the German theosophical movement by attending such events as the 1907 Munich Congress. Finally, after five years of studying, she was qualified in July 1911 as a medical doctor by Zurich University.

Over the next few years she worked in one of the Zurich general hospitals and then in another clinic, and by 1917 she had gained enough experience to open her own Zurich practice. By this time the centre of Rudolf Steiner's activities had also moved over into Switzerland and during the First World War she began to ask him for advice in particular medical cases. In the course of 1919 there arose in her the decision to move her own work to the Dornach neighbourhood, and in the following year—when the first anthroposophical medical course was also being given—she dissolved her Zurich practice and bought a house in Arlesheim, which opened in 1921 under the name of Clinical-Therapeutical Institute.

Rudolf Steiner responded to this initiative by himself now coming regularly for medical consultations with Wegman in the Institute. And so from this time onwards the collaboration between the two of them grew more and more intense. When the Goetheanum went up in flames during New Year's night of 1922/3 the seed was finally born in her that led to her direct question at Penmaenmawr in the following summer as to whether the mystery-principle in medicine could not be placed more in the foreground. To this question Rudolf Steiner replied that the medicine of the mysteries should be renewed. They then began to work together on the book later published as *Fundamentals of Therapy*. At the Christmas Foundation Meeting at the end of the year Ita Wegman was chosen by Rudolf Steiner as the Recorder of the esoteric *Vorstand* of the refounded Anthroposophical Society, and with reference to its newly initiated School of Spiritual

Science she was appointed to the leadership of the Medical Section. He was all too visibly placing her in a position of seemingly indisputable prominence. It must therefore also here be mentioned that already during Rudolf Steiner's lifetime a marked animosity towards Ita Wegman began to arise inside certain anthroposophical circles.

Throughout the year 1924 Wegman was present in the new capacities with which Rudolf Steiner had endowed her at almost all of his lectures both at Dornach and abroad. As the summer went on and he rose to the phenomenal peak of his lecturing activity he came increasingly to rely on her to support his ailing physical condition. After giving his last address on Michaelmas eve he withdrew to his sick bed where she then looked after him for the next six months. During this time she was in consequence closer to him than was any other person, and was among those present when he died at the end of March 1925.

Now among other activities during the last year of his life Rudolf Steiner had been writing for the anthroposophical news-sheet an inspiring weekly series entitled 'Leading Thoughts', of which the final number did not come out until a fortnight after his death. When a few more weeks had passed by, Ita Wegman took the initiative of in some sense continuing the series. It was the first time that she had written articles in her life, and they were composed in an impulsive, spontaneous manner—like letters to a friend, as her biographer remarks. In several of them she also interwove passages from meditations given to her personally by Rudolf Steiner and which at the time were unknown to anybody else. But she had not written more than three of these articles before a serious opposition to them on the part of some members began to make itself felt. (In this connection it is also interesting to note that the German word *Leitsätze* actually means 'leading sentences', in English an odd-sounding expression bearing little if any meaning. Consequently, in his translations of Rudolf Steiner's articles, George Adams had more suitably rendered it by the version 'Leading Thoughts', the literal German translation of which, *Leitgedanken*, Wegman herself then substituted for *Leitsätze* when

she realized the offence that was being taken by a part of her
readership. But even this change of name availed nothing.)
Her *Vorstand* colleague Albert Steffen, editor of the news-
sheet wherein these articles were appearing, joined in the
opposition to them, with the inevitable result that after a few
months this fascinating series, although of considerably
greater interest than much else published in the news-sheet
at that time, was simply discontinued.

Nor was this the only matter causing controversy within the
Anthroposophical Society in the months after Rudolf Steiner's death. One other such matter concerned the continuation of the First Class of the School of Spiritual Science. In
September 1924 Rudolf Steiner had indicated to many new
members of this Class that Wegman would be leading the
'Michael School' with him, and in November he told Count
Polzer-Hoditz that when the First Class was completely
formed it would be put into Wegman's hands. But as events
then turned out her appointment as its leader was never
formalized. On the basis of indications that Rudolf Steiner
had made to her Wegman felt herself appointed by the
spiritual world to continue the work of the Class as surviving
and secondary leader and protector of its mantras. With the
agreement of the whole *Vorstand* though at the same time to
the discomfiture of Marie Steiner, who would have been
leader of the Second Class had this ever been founded,
Wegman began to take Class Lessons, first in Paris and
then in Dornach and elsewhere. Those members who were
already hostile to her were quick to decry this as tantamount
to an arrogant claim on her part to be not only sole leader of
the School but also in effect the self-appointed 'possible
successor' of Rudolf Steiner referred to in Statute 7 of the
Anthroposophical Society. Ita Wegman herself never made
any such claims.

While these and other troublesome matters were proceeding on their rather convoluted course, Wegman was also
deeply occupied in building up further the medical work
that was her designated professional field. Under her guidance during these same years the Arlesheim clinic steadily
developed from very modest beginnings into a thriving and

organic centre for anthroposophical medicine wherein both training and practical therapy struggled through their pioneering phase and slowly began to establish themselves in the world at large. Qualified doctors, medical students, nurses, pharmaceutical researchers, dieticians, therapists, curative teachers and eurythmists, to say nothing of patients, passed constantly through its doors, gaining there fellowship, understanding, experience and healing, and then carrying its inspiration far and wide into other lands where numerous other clinics, curative homes and medical centres also came into being as daughter enterprises. Arlesheim was the recognizable source from which the healing impulses of anthroposophical medicine could flow out in a manifold network of interconnected streams for the lasting benefit of both mankind and the Earth itself.

Ita Wegman took the most active part in ensuring that the influence of this work would penetrate as deeply as possible into all those around her, primarily through warmth of human contact freely proferred to total newcomers and then continually renewed in a growing circle of friends with whom it was often underpinned by an extensive correspondence. Professional intercommunication in the more medical field was further stimulated by such enterprises as the journal *Natura*, which she founded in 1926 and edited thereafter. As a tireless traveller she also seized every opportunity to develop Anthroposophy especially in the West—in Holland and in England. She was deeply engaged in the World Conference on Spiritual Science held in London in 1928, and also in the Kamp de Stakenberg in Holland in 1929. Both of these initiatives, however, added fuel to the criticism of Wegman and her supporters inside the anthroposophical circles opposing her. With regard to the first, it was maintained that such a large-scale enterprise on the European periphery was effectively detracting from the importance of Dornach as the centre of the Anthroposophical Movement; as for the second, it was held in too unconventional a manner for anthroposophists of a less open-minded character.

So already by the beginning of the 1930s the particular style of Ita Wegman's engagement in positive anthroposophical

work had come to form a rallying point for some and a
stumbling stone for others. At Dornach the *Vorstand* had
anyway ceased to present a united front or to function
properly at all. In 1932—the year also of the opening of the
medical house at Kent Terrace in London—Wegman undertook a journey through Greece and the former Asia Minor.
Under the darkening political clouds of 1933 she redoubled
her activities especially in England, which she visited that year
no fewer than eight times. In the spring of the following year
she fell seriously ill and it was thought advisable to take her
high up into the Swiss Alps, where she remained for over six
months. When finally her health had improved she decided to
recuperate by going on another long journey, this time to
Palestine, so it was the end of the year before she at last
returned again to her work at Arlesheim.

In her lengthy absence the two conflicting sides in the
Anthroposophical Society had now arrived at a total breach.
The final seal was set on this in April 1935, at the Annual
General Meeting at Dornach, under the influence of a cam-
paign of lurid polemics mounted by her opponents in the
preceding months. Already tabled motions to expel Ita Wegman from the Society along with her principal supporters and
to sever the Anthroposophical Societies in both Holland and
Great Britain were carried by an overwhelming majority of
such members as had both felt inclined and been able to be
present.

From this time onwards Wegman clearly bore with her
something of the strange aura of a spiritual exile. Although
excluded from the Goetheanum, she continued her own work
at Arlesheim as before, maintaining both meetings and extensive correspondence with the network of doctors, curative
educators and other people in many lands who remained
faithful to her. Yet conditions became now in several respects
increasingly difficult. Her great friend D.N. Dunlop had died,
her visits to England became fewer, and public appearances in
Germany were now made impossible by the political scenery.
Only with the growing work in France did she make notable
further headway in a westerly direction. Interesting journeys
further afield during this period also took her to Iceland in

1936, Sicily in 1938 and, finally, to Bulgaria in the summer of 1939.

It was shortly after her return from this last journey abroad that the Second World War broke out. Within a few months the particular network of international anthroposophical connections of which Arlesheim had been the pulsating centre was for the duration simply shattered. The clinic itself turned largely into a stopping-place for refugees. In 1940 Wegman herself moved permanently away and settled at the Casa Andrea Cristoforo, a dependency of the Arlesheim clinic which she had founded in 1936 at Ascona on the shore of Lago Maggiore, near the Italian border. Here she lived for the last three years of her life, perforce very isolated by comparison with the previous years, but as energetic and creative as ever within the Casa itself and its immediate surroundings.

Towards the end of February 1943 she happened to be making a return visit to the clinic at Arlesheim. Suddenly she fell ill and she died there within a week, on 4 March—according to one who was present 'in full consciousness, and in deepest devotion and surrender to the spiritual world'.

The only obituaries to appear anywhere at all were both in British publications; that by George Adams in *Anthroposophical Movement*, and that by Adam Bittleston in *Christian Community Monthly Letter*.

⋆   ⋆   ⋆

The theme of the present volume is sufficiently indicated by its sub-title. (Although accepted for this series of esoteric studies, the collection does also include some reports of anthroposophical activities of a more exoteric character.) The volume draws more extensively on the articles published in German in the selection *An die Freunde* than it does on anything else, but is not the equivalent of that work. Various articles in *An die Freunde* which are of less direct relevance to the theme have been left out, but on the other hand other articles from the 1925–27 period absent from *An die Freunde* have been included. For although some of these are indeed reproduced in the third volume of the biographical documentation it seems also right that they should be allowed to stand in something more approaching the context of the whole article-series of which they were designed to form part. The same considerations apply with regard to the various passages which were omitted from some of the articles in *An die Freunde*; these are here all fully restored. Also included are, firstly, the longer article from *Natura*, 'The Being of Man and the Season of Michaelmas', which is naturally related to the theme; and secondly, the report of the 1928 World Conference on Spiritual Science, for this Conference, as explained by Wegman herself, stood in intimate connection to the impulse of the Summer Schools, which was clearly set in a Michaelic context in her announcement of that at Gareloch one year previously. Having thereby brought the volume to focus on London, it seemed only appropriate to continue it with the two addresses which Wegman gave in that capital on Rudolf Steiner's birthday in the years 1931 and 1933. From a whole decade later comes the obituary of Wegman by George Adams, which provides a suitable conclusion by drawing attention to the theme of the Michael Impulse in relation to Ita Wegman's own life.

The chief basis of the texts here presented is formed by the original translations previously referred to in this Foreword. These appeared in *Anthroposophical Movement* simultaneously with the appearance of their originals in *Was in der Anthroposophischen Gesellschaft vorgeht* on the given dates, apart from the report of the World Conference which appeared in English one week later, and 'The Being of Man and the Season of Michaelmas', which did not appear in English until its inclusion in the Michaelmas 1932 number of *Anthroposophy*. For the present edition the articles have been recollated with their originals. Who it was who translated all these articles of Wegman's is nowhere stated, but the natural supposition that it was George Adams himself (who indeed refers to the 1925 series in his obituary of Wegman) is certainly given support by the peculiarly felicitous manner in which various quite intractable passages in the German have been rendered into an elegant English equivalent. Nonetheless, I have felt justified in making numerous revisions and improvements throughout, and therefore take responsibility for the accuracy of the final versions.

The address on Rudolf Steiner from 1931 exists in four drafts discovered in four different places, and conflated together for the first volume of the biographical documentation, where it appears as an appendix. But its interest is so great that it surely deserves a rather more suitable and available setting, so I have translated this conflated version and included it in the present collection.

The address on the same subject in 1933 was the chief occasion on which Wegman decided to relate something of her life, and is of paramount importance in the reconstruction of certain parts of her biography. Hitherto only the draft of the address has been made available. Its first part was published in 1945 in the memorial volume *Erinnerungen an Ita Wegman*, which has since then gone into further impressions. In 1947 this book was translated into English as *Memories of Ita Wegman*; it has never since been reprinted and is now in consequence a rare item. For the first volume of the documentation the same part of the draft was then republished as an appendix, with the rest of it—previously not generally known—being incorporated into one of the chapters. But this address may also suitably be allowed to stand as a whole in the form in which it was actually delivered, for the text of the address here presented is not that of the previously published draft but of a hitherto unpublished typescript from the library of Rudolf Steiner House, London. While following the main course of the draft the typescript nonetheless also contains various short passages not found in the draft, some of considerable interest. Contrariwise, certain interesting variants and short passages recorded in the draft but not appearing in the typescript have here also been included in brackets.

The obituary of Wegman by George Adams first appeared in *Anthroposophical Movement* in the issue of the given months, and was reprinted, with certain omissions and alterations, in both the German and English versions of *Memories of Ita Wegman*. It is here republished in its original form, with slight corrections.

This Foreword cannot properly end without an expression

of my thanks to Margaret Jonas for orientation in the library at Rudolf Steiner House, to my sister Clare for putting me up in her London home, and, above all, to my wife Charlotte for creating the atmosphere around me in which it was possible to work on this book.

It was in London on 2 May 1913 that Rudolf Steiner spoke for the first time of the Archangel Michael as the inspiring guide of our present historic age. Towards the end of the lecture he gave on this subject to the small band of his earliest English followers he included the following observation: 'And even if many people do not recognize this new Michael revelation, it will nonetheless spread out over mankind.' May this present volume inspire those who do indeed recognize such a revelation to further its spread within the English-speaking world to which Ita Wegman showed herself so closely connected.

Crispian Villeneuve
Devon
February 1993

In Memory of the Christmas Foundation Meeting

26 April 1925

In full consciousness, but without a word spoken of the future, without having left any messages or instructions for this or that person, the Master departed from us. And to a direct question in this regard he consciously answered 'No'. Why was this?

The Christmas Foundation Meeting, a decisive event for the Anthroposophical Society, stands clear before our minds. No member who took part in it can fail to have been convinced that with this Meeting the Anthroposophical Society received a deepening and a direction whereby, in relation to what had gone before, a new and independent starting-point was created. Henceforth it was not just the Anthroposophical Society alone; the Anthroposophical Movement itself was now within it. For Rudolf Steiner, the leader of the Anthroposophical Movement, working with new energy, with unheard-of vitality, inspired by fresh impulses, had now fused it with the Anthroposophical Society, which previously was separate from the Movement, with its own administration and its own *Vorstand*. From this moment onward—25 December 1923—there arose a new karma for the Anthroposophical Society. To what it possessed of old, something new was added: Rudolf Steiner henceforth identified himself with the Society!

Did each member at that time really take hold of what was happening, really grasp that from now onward everyone had new and deep responsibilities to bear? Did each one understand what a sacrificial deed had taken place? Rudolf Steiner received the karma of the Anthroposophical Society into his

own karma. It was an unheard-of venture; when the deed took
place, one could almost feel the whole cosmos quiver in
response. How gladly and bounteously hitherto the spiritual
powers had poured out spiritual knowledge over the Anthroposophical Movement, which was Rudolf Steiner himself—
poured it out so that this knowledge could also be spoken
about, and spoken about just in the way it was! Whether they
would act with the same benevolence towards the Anthroposophical Society now depended on this historic moment.
Leadership of the Anthroposophical Society entails administration; in the Society the wishes, the thoughts, the will of
members are expressed. Is it possible for light from the
spiritual world to flow through these with the same power
and intensity? That was the anxious question, and one had to
wait and see how things would further evolve.

Meanwhile, the Meeting took its course most wonderfully.
Rudolf Steiner appointed the *Vorstand* for the Society. This
Vorstand was chosen by him with the Michael Impulse, and
was so organized that it would be possible for him to work
with it. Not the Society, but he, Rudolf Steiner, appointed the
Vorstand, explaining that this *Vorstand* stood in inner connection with himself; he therefore called it esoteric.

This was clearly expressed, and the Anthroposophical
Society, which had sent its members in so large a number
to the Meeting, certainly grasped the full import of the
situation. Fired with enthusiasm, it gave its full agreement,
and many, indeed most of its members promised sacredly to
themselves to enter into the new arrangement and serve the
Master with renewed strength, with a new feeling and a new
will.

A wave of true enthusiasm was kindled. Something great
had happened. Each person felt this; consciously or unconsciously, this feeling was there. But there still stood before us
the anxious question: how will the spirit take its further
course? And to this question too there came one day the
answer. It was moving to hear this answer from Rudolf
Steiner's own lips.

This was in Paris, when for the first time he was able to give
this most important message to the members present there,

who were only gathered in a small number—the message that
the stream of spiritual revelations had not ceased to flow, and
that the spiritual powers had bestowed their spiritual gifts on
the Anthroposophical Society with still greater benevolence
than before. How the tension was suddenly relieved! And
what jubilation and happiness there was! The spiritual powers
are well inclined towards us, because the Christmas Foundation Meeting was received in the right spirit by the members.
How radiant was our Master's face! How overjoyed he himself
was! How thankful were his faithful pupils who sat gathered
around him in the small but beautiful room in Paris! And now
the truths flowed mightily from his lips. More and more he
gave. The glad message, spoken for the first time in Paris, he
repeated in Dornach, Torquay, London and in Holland, and
important truths from the spiritual world were given. It was as
though the floodgates from the spiritual world were opened,
to let the spiritual wealth flow out. An unforgettable time!
Everybody felt himself uplifted, felt himself daily in a festal
mood; it was also as though the Gods themselves were
celebrating a festival.

The time was short but intense in its effects. Everybody
who had partaken in the right way in the Christmas Meeting,
the Michael Meeting, could experience in himself how he
became transformed, how he became another man, how the
spiritual world had come quite near; indeed, one found
oneself within it.

Then the Master was taken ill. To begin with, it was but
bodily exhaustion, but later on the causes of the illness were
shown to lie deeper: karma was working itself out. From
January 1925 onwards, he no longer spoke of exhaustion but
of the workings of karma. Oh, may the members not pass such
expressions by! They are to be taken in real earnest.

Now he left the physical plane, and, in addition to what
there was before, he left us what was newly voiced in the
Christmas Meeting, what had given rise to new situations and
made new groupings necessary.

All that he had intended to regulate, and about which he
had spoken in the various conferences after the Christmas
Meeting, could still be settled in the last two months of his

life, so that by a stroke of good fortune the proper settlement of the business side of things was still possible shortly before his death. And so he was able to leave his physical body without considering it necessary to leave any further instructions for the guidance of the Anthroposophical Society.

To us whom he had chosen as *Vorstand*, it was clear that we must not desert our posts, which had been designated by him. It was clear to us that it was a sacred duty—if we took in real earnest what the Master has transmitted to us from the spiritual world—to remain grouped around him, in order that he, though he could no longer be among us physically, might yet be able to work among us and in us. This was the feeling that held sway in us. And so we still regard Rudolf Steiner as President within our *Vorstand*, and all members of the *Vorstand* as having the functions to which Rudolf Steiner appointed them.

May the members come to meet us with the same feelings as we cherish for the Society, so that we may actively work on and on according to the intentions of our leader Rudolf Steiner, and bring to effect the legacy of the Christmas Foundation Meeting.

The Old Goetheanum and the New

3 May 1925

When the Goetheanum was taken from us by the disastrous conflagration of 1922, and we stood in deep distress around our teacher Rudolf Steiner, yet still able to gather strength from him, we did not imagine that two-and-a-half years later he himself, our adviser and our most faithful friend, would leave us. Painfully wounded as we were, we found support and comfort in the purposeful way he went straight forward and in his composed manner. Soon we found ourselves strengthened afresh, found our place in the new situation, and rallied around him with re-quickened forces. True, we no longer possessed the Goetheanum on the physical plane, but spiritually it still stood there, spiritually we were united with it. We absolutely had to be united with it, for we were also united to such a great extent and in so intensive a way with the creator of this work of art, Rudolf Steiner.

There lies a mystery in this: to be at once creator of this work of art, and Rudolf Steiner! How does a man become creator of a work of art? The God in him builds geometrically a structure all around him from ethereal substance, and he himself stands in the midst of this structure. Then he need but reproduce externally this work of art built of ethereal substance, and the work of art stands complete on the physical plane. The 'Word' ethereally moulds the geometric forms, and from these geometric-ethereal forms the physical forms result and are reproduced artistically in physical material. Thus the Goetheanum arose out of Rudolf Steiner. His Word, which proclaimed Anthroposophy, built the Goetheanum ethereally. It was the condensed Word of Rudolf Steiner, and his own ether body was coalesced with this work of art, bound up with it inseparably.

What then happened with the fire? Once more a mystery took place among us. With the destruction of the Goetheanum on the physical plane, Rudolf Steiner's spiritual members were loosed from his physical body and the possibility arose that he too, the Master, would leave us on the physical plane. But this was not to happen; Rudolf Steiner had to stay. The success of his spiritual task, pictured in its earthly accomplishment, had not yet reached the point where his pupils would have been ready to carry this earthly accomplishment forward. So the Master remained, but not as an ordinary man whose physical body is intimately united with the higher members; he remained as a man who had his spiritual members altogether in the spiritual world, from where he but directed his physical body. He became thereby freer and more mighty, but his physical body became weaker and more brittle.

The question arises in us: if the Goetheanum had not been destroyed, what then would have happened? Yes, if the destruction had not taken place, if this sacrifice had not been offered up, then we might perhaps have lost our master and leader, Rudolf Steiner—he might then have become the sacrifice. When after the fire this possibility began to be felt, a tremendous sense of thanks was mingled with the sadness. We still had our friend and teacher in our midst, our support was still there, indeed he was even freer and mightier among us. For this we could be glad and still inwardly thankful.

Through his strong will he mastered his weakened physical body. One can scarcely form a conception of this superhuman will without an overall picture of the fulness of his work in the last years. How infinitely much he gave! A stream of revelations opened out and inaugurated a new cultural life.

But now the Goetheanum was to be built up again—this was the wish of the whole Anthroposophical Society, to have a building for Anthroposophy and all that is connected with it. But it was also clear that the Goetheanum could not be built up again in the way it was before, at least not by Rudolf Steiner. Copied it might have been, but not creatively repeated.

Only after the Christmas Foundation Meeting could

Rudolf Steiner concern himself intensively with the thought of the new building. This new Goetheanum had to be connected with the Michael Impulses, had to be a castle of Michael where Michael's pupils could find themselves together, and come together to hear the message of Michael. It had to be like a castle so as to withstand the onslaught of adversary powers, built of firm material, artistic and beautiful, yet severe and strong in its forms and lines. It had to be erected at the behest of the Archangel Michael, which he gave to his subordinate helpers in the spiritual world. The right moment had to be awaited. In the spiritual world the new Goetheanum had to appear; only then was it possible to bring it down onto the physical plane. And this was done on our behalf by Rudolf Steiner.

This festal moment came, as I said, after the Christmas Foundation Meeting—unforgettable for those who were privileged to experience it.

When the time had come, the Master put on his white overall, ordered the prepared clay, and began to shape the model of the new Goetheanum. He worked feverishly, without any real pause for rest. I was privileged to be present and witnessed with astonishment, with a holy awe, how the model came into being. In three days it was finished, and then it stood there, unique in its severe, mighty, and yet so beautiful forms. From this model we are now to erect the new Goetheanum on the Dornach hill, a building for the Anthroposophy of the present and the future! Anthroposophy, with its friends and opponents, needs a building that will do justice to both, a building in whose inner spaces men can devote themselves to art, and can hear the Word that Anthroposophy would proclaim—a building which outwardly in its form and resistant material will bear witness to its purpose, to stand fast and to protect.

Castle of Michael, new Goetheanum!

Radiantly happy, the Master stood beside his model. When this model had been carried across from the Studio to the Glasshouse for the preparation of the plans, he said to me: 'It caused some sensation when the model was carried from the Studio to its second workshop, the Glasshouse.' How indeed can it be otherwise, when miracles take place before men's eyes!

May we all help, so that this second Goetheanum, prepared with so much love, with so much effort, yes, even perhaps with the sacrifice of his own health, may be erected in all its greatness and glory to the honour of its great Master, Rudolf Steiner.

To All Members!

17 May 1925

It was of a deepening of Anthroposophy, of a new direction in the Anthroposophical Movement, that Rudolf Steiner spoke during the Christmas Foundation Meeting, and in the period that followed it. What did he mean by this? He spoke of the Stream of Michael that wishes to make itself felt through Anthroposophy in earthly evolution, to bring forth its own life in Anthroposophy. A permeation of Earth existence with the power and will of Michael is what had to take place. And so it is of immense importance that all anthroposophical spiritual knowledge, which for so many years past was brought down from the spirit world with such courage, such tremendous freshness and energy by the spiritual investigator Rudolf Steiner, should be consciously united with this Stream of Michael. The deepening of which Rudolf Steiner spoke is this: to become conscious of Michael's working into Anthroposophy. Illumined by the new Impulses of Michael, a mighty picture must arise of all anthroposophical spirit-knowledge. It must be lifted out of all sectarian activity and implanted in the all-embracing world activity that is always connected with Michael. There must not arise in the Society separate islands where Anthroposophy is taught but where one might forget to emphasize the permeation of this knowledge with the Michael Impulses.

If these islands arise and the work of Michael is not consciously received into the hearts of men and understood, then the danger will arise that the anthroposophical teachings will in a short time be made superficial, and Ahriman, working in human beings, will take possession of this knowledge and the Anthroposophical Society will be robbed of it.

Why is Michael so important for us? Through Rudolf
Steiner we know that Michael, who previously ruled over
the cosmic intellectuality, had to give this intellectuality away
during the course of Earth evolution, because the freedom
that had to come in human evolution requires this intellectuality in man himself. But Michael knows that with the
intellectuality in man there also arise great dangers for him.
Therefore what unfolds as intelligence in man he wishes to
maintain in continuous connection with the divine-spiritual
beings. For if this is not done, the great danger will arise that
Ahrimanic beings, aware of the fact that it has been loosed and
severed from the Gods, will absorb this intelligence and unite
it with themselves. They would thereby become the mightiest
intelligences in the cosmos.

Michael knows these dangers very well, knows moreover
that man has not yet the faculties to recognize these dangers
and that if he were now to meet with Ahriman he would
necessarily fall a victim to him. Hence Michael holds the
Ahrimanic powers beneath his feet, driving them continually
back into a subhuman world to which man, if he develops in
the right way, finds no access. Thus Ahriman is held in check
by Michael, and this activity, this process, is expressed in
human consciousness as a mighty picture—the picture of the
Dragon with whom Michael does battle, driving him into the
abyss. The perpetual anxiety of Michael is: will he be able to
hold men away from Ahriman? Will men really grasp the
Christ-Being, who has descended onto the Earth, and follow
Him? The whole treasure of Anthroposophy is a Christ-filled
wisdom of the cosmos. By the mediation of the mighty spirit-
being in Rudolf Steiner it came onto the Earth; men have
received it.

Weak human hands are guarding it; human intellectuality
as it grows strong can bring it into danger.

Hitherto Rudolf Steiner was in the midst of men. It was his
earthly task to bring the wisdom of Christ to men who have
been taken hold of by intellectuality, so that through this
wisdom he might bring them on in evolution to the point
when they would recognize the Christ and follow Him, and
thus be able to do battle with Ahriman. Step by step he led

them on, instilling wisdom, while Michael, step by step, set the intellectuality free. Together they went forward, for the healing of mankind, guarding and giving.

Michael came ever nearer to humanity and is now working as a real power among men. The Christmas Foundation Meeting spoke of this. The Meeting spoke of Anthroposophy being the treasures of wisdom of those Gods whom Michael serves. It spoke of the cosmic and human intellectuality, which is Michael's gift to man. All of this is now there for those human beings who have an open heart and a good will.

But human beings are hovering in danger. Anti-Michael powers are ready to absorb the intelligences of men, to darken the wisdom of the Gods, robbing it of its depth, so that the divine forces may no longer be able to wield their influence, nor human beings able to understand the cosmic wisdom.

Closed now are the human lips which brought us this wisdom of the Gods. They can no longer warn and guide us in human language.

We must take earnestly what he said, what he placed in the very centre of Anthroposophy: the Stream of Michael. *Michael is with human beings the Guardian of Anthroposophy.* May a sufficient number of people become conscious of the active power that Michael is among mankind. May all those who have the strength and courage, not only to bring the Michael-thought to manifestation in their souls but to make it living in their deeds, become true servants of Michael and bring about his victory, and thus lead mankind over the great crisis with which it is now confronted.

Then too there will come together that number of persons of whom our great leader spoke, whom he required to accomplish his own and Michael's intentions. This number will come together, inspired to action by their conscience, for in conscience the highest Gods speak their own language.

They will be prompted to declare themselves inwardly as servants of Michael, in Time and Eternity, in the love of the Gods, in the heights of the cosmos.

Leading Thoughts

1 Michael, through his activity, is closely united with man, and having given the cosmic intelligence to man, he seeks to maintain his connection with it.

2 Michael becomes the Guardian of Anthroposophy, because he hopes to find in it those human beings who will *serve* him, and because with their service it is his will to guard Anthroposophy until the great teacher comes back again.

3 All anthroposophical spirit-knowledge must be grouped in living rays around the Stream of Michael, and deepened through the consciousness of being connected with him.

To All Members!

24 May 1925

If Michael is to be the Guardian of Anthroposophy, then what must the human beings who would serve him bring as an offering to him?

Through Rudolf Steiner, we know that Michael endeavours in all earnestness to help men that they may unfold to the full the flower of the humanity within them. As a servant of the divine-spiritual powers of the second and third Hierarchies Michael in the past administered the cosmic intellectuality. When this cosmic intellectuality was loosed from the divine-spiritual powers, so that it might find its way to man, it was Michael's will to work on entirely in the sense of those powers and to remain their servant. He resolved to enter into a right relationship to mankind, and therefore he wished to pour intellectuality into man as the very same force that it had been within the divine-spiritual powers, permeated with the forces of love. It was his intention that men should not only have intellectuality in their head but an intellectuality also that streams through the heart. He combined intellectuality with the warm and intimate life of the soul that lay in his own nature, and in that of the divine-spiritual powers. And with this intellectuality of the heart he wished to kindle in man a love for the world. Love for the world can only be possessed by the man who has rightly united the intellectuality of head and heart within him. Once this love is there, it will radiate back into one's own self, and one will be able to love without falling into self-love. This indicates the way that leads to Christ.

Michael would lead men to Christ, and he looks for those who will champion his cause.

Anthroposophy, too, which is a wisdom of the Gods, would prepare the souls of men to find the Christ.

The Age of Michael has dawned once again. An understanding of this fact must be awakened in man. Michael's nature must be understood. Again and again Rudolf Steiner said this to those who were willing to hear him. First he announced in his lectures the working of Michael, who as Archangel took over the leadership from Gabriel in the year 1879. Then followed the lectures to awaken our understanding to a living grasp of Michael, and finally there followed those lectures that spoke of Michael's connection with Anthroposophy. In mighty pictures there were revealed to us the former epochs of Michael's dominion, the last of which was in the time from 601 to 247 BC, and the last but one in the Gilgamesh period of the Chaldean cultural epoch.

At the beginning of Michael's last regency there stood in the centre of the civilized life of that time the work of Aristotle, and intimately connected with it were the campaigns of Alexander. In Aristotle there flowed the wisdom of Plato, which was the wisdom of the Eleusinian Mysteries. The knowledge of nature which Aristotle possessed came through a natural science that reached up to Heaven in order to understand the earthly world, and which had flowed out of the wisdom-treasures of the Chthonic and Eleusinian Mysteries. For this natural science in ancient Greece the time had passed. There were no more men to understand it in the right way. It could only be saved by Aristotle becoming the teacher of Alexander. Alexander received this science into himself, and through his campaigns into Asia he carried all that was possible of the Aristotelian science to the East. There it passed over into the Jewish and Arabian Schools. Later on it was led through Africa into Spain, and filtered in through the European life of learning, entering into relation with individual human beings in central Europe and extending right up to Ireland in the Mysteries of Hibernia. It was Alexander's deed to break forth from the small and narrow national frontiers of his land into the wide world, taking with him the Aristotelian wisdom and scholarship. In all his campaigns he lived it. It was living in him, and with it he penetrated wherever he went. He was strongly imbued with the Michael Impulse—the impulse to battle for an idea and to carry it far away beyond the frontiers of one's own land; he was a cosmopolitan. He had to go forth as a conqueror of foreign lands so as to be able to implant new impulses in old cultures. It was not for his own sake but for the glorification of Aristotle that he undertook his great campaigns; the purpose of his campaigns in foreign lands was to make the teachings of Aristotle known throughout the world.

This heroic spirit, this acting out of love and being given up entirely to the impulses of the divine-spiritual powers was the delight of Michael, said Rudolf Steiner. Hence the unparalleled successes in the youthful and fiery progress of Alexander, who was fearless and did things scarcely possible to man.

It was in that Age of Michael that the Mystery Centre of Ephesus also blossomed forth. How inspiringly did Rudolf Steiner speak of the significance of the Ephesian Mysteries for the Goetheanum, for the newly kindling life of the Dornach Mystery Centre, showing us how the fire of the Goetheanum brought with it the deepest revelations, which are to be read in the Fire-Akasha of that memorable New Year's Eve and point to the ancient temple of Ephesus, the house of the goddess Diana, which was also the victim of conflagration. He described how in Ephesus the Mystery of the Logos was taught; he described how the secrets of the macrocosm can be felt when we understand the living Word in man as microcosm. The Mysteries of Ephesus, too, stood beneath the Impulse of Michael. There was a great impulse of freedom in these wisdom teachings. To these Mysteries not only men but women had access, and strangers alien to the land, if they were mature enough, were admitted—customs that were not possible in other centres of the ancient mysteries. Moreover, in Ephesus the first impulse was given for the development of human personality.

Thus the Michael Impulse is clearly marked out in Ephesus, through Aristotle, Alexander, and on to the Goetheanum. Now we stand once more under the Sign of Michael. We possess Anthroposophy, but we have lost our dear and faithful leader and the Goetheanum, which was created out of his very being and built by him.

What must we now do, if with Michael we would guard Anthroposophy? How must we act if we are not to lose the leadership of our Master from the spiritual worlds, so that Anthroposophy can put forth its fresh blossoms?

Dear friends, we must bring to Michael the readiness, out of freedom and without falling a victim to egoism, to work in love. We must take hold of freedom in its true greatness. Anthroposophy must become even more than hitherto cosmopolitan, must not be bottled up by groups of people nor remain limited to special countries. It is for everyone throughout the whole world. That is Michael's will. He will have love for the world spread over all mankind.

Make yourselves ready, you younger friends, you who are ensouled with fire, you who have courage, who have intellectuality not only in your heads but also in your hearts, make yourselves ready to place yourselves under the Sign of Michael, to follow and to serve him.

Leading Thoughts

1 The connections between the Michael Impulses given in the different Michael Ages are plainly recognizable. To the impulse of freedom and the cosmopolitan development of mankind is now added that of intellectuality, which must not only include the head but the heart also, so that the humanity in man may come to full development.

2 All narrow, sectarian covering-up of Wisdom's treasure is foreign to Michael; he wants to bestow his treasures on everyone in the whole world who has the will to serve and follow him.

3 Anthroposophy, therefore, if it does not wish to lose from out of the spiritual world the leadership of its Master, who only has what is truly great in view, must free itself from all pettiness.

To All Members!

7 June 1925

If a man is willing to serve Michael he must approach him actively. Michael cannot be reached in passive devotion or in prayerful mood, but one reaches him by placing oneself actively within the spiritual. With one's will one rallies to his hosts.

And since Michael is very closely bound up with mankind, because he has to govern the spiritual forces in mankind and the revelation of the divine intellect, one finds him living in that part of the spiritual world that is only separated from the physical world by a thin veil.

In a most moving way Rudolf Steiner tells us about himself, how in the seventies and eighties of the last century he was living with his intellectual soul outside the physical world, in this spiritual world separated by so thin a wall from the physical world—a world in which Michael and his hosts were also living. He said that in this world, to which man cannot penetrate with his ordinary consciousness, things of tremendous import were taking place around Michael. Powerful adherents of Michael were there, human souls passing through the life between death and a new birth, but also there were powerful demonic beings who wanted to hinder what was to be brought into the world through Michael.

Michael, who is a God of the Sun Mysteries, living in the Sun, came down as far as the ethereal world when the time again dawned for his Earth mission, his rulership, so as to be able to approach man as nearly as might be. In the future, his will is to set up his dwelling in the hearts and souls of earthly men.

He needs the spiritual trust of humanity. If he has this trust he will work as the inspirer of men. It is easy for those who live intensely in the intellectual soul and then unite themselves with Michael to attain to the world where he lives and to receive his inspirations.

Therefore it is so important that the young people who live in this Michael Age should know of his working. Many who feel in themselves the urge to come to Anthroposophy had lived during an earlier Michael Age on the Earth, or participated in the supersensible Michael School, or even had both of these experiences. Ignorance of Michael's mission and of his intentions, a will not to receive direction from the spiritual world, sleepiness or inattentiveness in face of the operations of the spiritual world, which manifest themselves so delicately, could become catastrophic for the evolution of man and of the Earth.

The world of spirits awaits with longing the approach of mankind; it waits with longing for the individual human being, feeling himself as a soul of light, to grasp the world of spirits with his arms of light, and surrender himself to it.

The elemental beings also await their redemption and awakening through man. When man's aid does not come they feel themselves in danger of coming to the realm of the Dragon, of Ahriman. They are filled with uneasiness. Above and around man, everywhere there is movement.

To a chosen group of people treasures of wisdom were given by the greatest leader of humanity and teacher upon the Earth. He proclaimed everything that can bring one further in evolution, everything that is a human duty; he proclaimed how the elemental spirits may be helped, how they in their turn can help; he proclaimed how the spiritual beings manifest themselves on Earth, how they work in man, how they hope to be understood by man.

The paths are made clear, the knowledge has been given; everywhere there is expectation, movement!

The leader looked on in sorrow. Mankind lay sunk in sleep. The anti-Michael demons stood by, sneering, ready to attack. We are at work, says their manner.

Clearer, more penetrating became the Master's speech.

The laws of karma were revealed. *Before* the Christmas
Foundation Meeting it was not possible to speak in so
penetrating a way about karma and its laws, for the Anthroposophical Society was then so formed that on account of its
resistances karma could not be spoken about, at least not so
profoundly as was the case *after* that Meeting. Because of the
resistance that met the occult teacher there arose a whole host
of demons hindering the utterance of karmic truths. The
revelation of the mysteries of karma is always exposed to the
strong resistance of the Ahrimanic powers, who want to wrap
karma in obscurity. These resistances had to be overcome if
the Anthroposophical Society were not to be severed from the
youth forces, from the Michael Impulses.

Then the miraculous thing happened which I have already
spoken about. The Master united his destiny with the Anthroposophical Society. The sacrifice was made purposefully and
consciously; the conditions were there for the sacrifice to take
place.

Even as the Christ-Being united Himself with the Earth for
the good of mankind, so did Rudolf Steiner identify himself
with the Anthroposophical Society. It was a Christ act.

A portion of Michael's enemies was silenced. It was possible to speak without reserve of the repeated earth lives of
personalities associated with Michael or opposing him. The
other portion of Michael's enemies will be vanquished when
karma is understood by men.

If karma is understood with the powers of the heart and
head, and the truth of repeated Earth lives is received without
emotion or frivolity, and understood in real earnest, then it
will also be possible to vanquish the last anti-Michael demons,
and the Michael Age will proceed together with the coming
Christ Event.

People, old and young, must join together. In accordance
with destiny they were brought together for the sake of mutual
understanding, mutual aid. Spiritual truths are always the
same whether they are revealed in ancient or modern times; it
is only the way in which they approach men, the way in which
men grasp them, that changes. We are living in the Age of
Michael, his speech is sounding to us, and everyone, whether

old or young, can hear it if he or she will. Let us flock around his banner!

May these be the redemptive thoughts of Whitsuntide. They are earnest ones, but also full of hope, because through our powers of knowledge we human beings can do something helpful for the understanding of the coming important events in the Michael Age!

Leading Thoughts

Michael may be reached when one places oneself actively in the spiritual; he cannot be reached through passive devotion or prayerful mood.

A great desire to help man prevails in the spiritual world, and impatience and expectation in the world of elemental beings for redemption by man. Above, below and around man there is movement; the divine-spiritual would proclaim itself.

To understand karma in connection with oneself and with others means to vanquish Ahrimanic powers. With the karma revelations the fight between Michael and Ahriman has begun.

To All Members!

14 June 1925

Rudolf Steiner's first visit to Paris after the War took place during 23–27 May 1924. This happened as the result of an invitation from the French Anthroposophical Society, founded in Paris, which recently has been developing so successfully under the initiative and leadership of the Secretary General, Mlle Sauerwein. After the Christmas Foundation Meeting in Dornach, at which the laying of the spiritual Foundation Stone of the General Anthroposophical Society took place, there followed the formation of the national Societies in the various countries, to which Rudolf Steiner was then invited. It was a solemn moment at the opening of the gathering when, after a long absence, the old French friends could once more have in their midst their beloved leader and master and hear him speak. This gathering made a deep impression on all who had the good fortune to be present.

In memory of this visit of Rudolf Steiner's, we, the *Vorstand* in Dornach, received an invitation to attend the General Meeting of the French Society, which had been fixed to take place on almost the same date this year. Dr Vreede and I, who had gone to the meeting in the previous year, were able to accept once more the invitation of the Paris friends. The gathering again took place in the beautiful little room in which, the year before, Rudolf Steiner's words had resounded.

The French Society is making very good progress, which can be confirmed by the fact that new members are constantly being announced, and the sale of Dr Steiner's books increases every day. Dr Steiner also praised the spirituality of our Paris friends, so that it was then possible for him to reveal important things in his lectures. Remembering the wonderful atmosphere that then prevailed, this present gathering passed off also in the fullest harmony.

On the first day I was able to deliver a short address with regard to the important event of the Christmas Foundation Meeting at Dornach. And I could once again let pass before the souls of our friends what had urged Rudolf Steiner to found the Anthroposophical Society anew, and to unite and identify his own person with it, whereas formerly he had only directed the Anthroposophical Movement. It is an absolute necessity that each individual member should grasp this fact in all its magnitude and significance. Dr Steiner referred me over and over again to the importance of the Christmas Meeting, and also to the fact that the hearts of the members were not nearly sufficiently permeated with it. For example, an unforgettable impression was made on me by his following statement: 'There is a discrepancy between my will, what is said out of this my will to the members, and what the members actually receive and understand.' This is not now the time to speak about these things in more detail; I just wished to insert this here in order to show that the importance of the Christmas Meeting is very far from being universally understood, since I often hear opinions to the effect that the Christmas Meeting should not always be placed so much in the foreground. I, however, am of the conviction that one cannot speak too often about the Christmas Foundation Meeting, that one cannot occupy oneself too much with the spiritual reasons that led to the laying anew of the Foundation Stone of the Anthroposophical Society.

I will now continue with the description of the Paris Conference. After my address, opportunity was given for questions to be asked, of which those present richly availed themselves, so that answers could be given on many important matters which were not at all clear in the minds of the members.

On the following day, the General Meeting of the French Society was opened by the Secretary General, Mlle Sauerwein. As always happens in such meetings, mutual dissatis-

factions were voiced, those of the members with the leadership, and those of the leadership with the members. It is good
that this should be done. Many things are thereby cleared up
which originate from misunderstandings, if one can only see
deeply enough into the souls of men. A generous spirit was
revealed by both parties during this discussion, which made a
deep impression on me. An honest will to understand each
other, and to work further together only in the spirit of our
great master and leader, Rudolf Steiner, whose presence we
really felt with us during this Meeting, came fully to expression. So the discussion ended in perfect harmony.

Dr Kolisko, who had joined us, was asked by the Secretary
General, Mlle Sauerwein, to give an address. He did this with
pleasure at the end of the General Meeting, and spoke about
Anthroposophy in general and about the new Leading
Thoughts. He was also able to visit the small eurythmy school
for children, directed by Mlle Rihouet, and in his capacity as a
doctor of the Medical Section he was able to occupy himself
in detail with the children, and give valuable advice to Mlle
Rihouet and the parents regarding the treatment of the little
ones. Unfortunately, I could not myself be present at this visit
because a number of the members wished to speak with me
personally, and as our time in Paris was limited I had to forego
it. Mlle Rihouet was, as always, full of life, and full of
enthusiasm for the tasks that devolve upon her. There is no
doubt that the work to which she has put her hand will be
carried forward in the right way.

In the evening Dr Vreede gave a lecture on Astronomy. In
the clear way we know so well, she brought near to us the
world of the stars in all its spirituality. Afterwards there was a
further opportunity for questions.

On Monday evening there was an esoteric lesson of the
First Class of the School of Spiritual Science at the Goetheanum, which had to be held by me.

With regard to the continuation of these class lessons the
following must be said. When our master, Rudolf Steiner, left
us on the physical plane, one of the most important questions
occupying the *Vorstand* was the continuation of the esoteric
teaching, which after the Christmas Foundation Meeting had

once more been brought so powerfully into the foreground of anthroposophical activity. It was clear to us that for the time being the thing to do was to guard the given esoteric teaching, and through repetition to bring the forces lying within this esoteric teaching to a living activity among the members.

When Dr Steiner founded this First Class of the free School of Spiritual Science he appointed me as his colleague. At that time the newly accepted pupils, those pupils who had received no esoteric teaching from earlier times, promised to be true members of the School. Therefore after the death of our teacher, Rudolf Steiner, I did not feel myself released from these commitments. On the contrary, I felt them more deeply than ever, for I have to look on the arrangements made by Dr Steiner as realities of the spiritual world. So there fell to me the task of repeating the esoteric lessons given by Dr Steiner for the School of Spiritual Science. And to my great satisfaction the first step towards this end could be taken in Paris. With this esoteric lesson, the Paris Conference was brought to a fitting close.

It only remains for me now to extend my heartfelt thanks to all those who worked for its success, especially the Secretary General, Mlle Sauerwein, who spared herself no trouble, and M. Jules Sauerwein, who with such devotion postponed pressing work of his own in order to be able to give the translation of the class lesson. My thanks are also due to all the members who contributed to the success of this Conference.

To All Members!

28 June 1925

Three attitudes of mind have been awakened in the members by the Leading Thoughts, which it was my wish to continue in the sense intended by Dr Steiner. Firstly, there has been a strongly positive affirmation, which has made itself known on all sides—a joyful and confident mood, which has turned to the *Vorstand* full of trust and ready to help in bearing the tremendous tasks that had to be undertaken by them after the death of our beloved master and leader. Secondly, there has been a negative attitude of scepticism taken up by a small group of people, who have opposed what desired to proceed courageously forward. Thirdly, a still smaller group have begun to find fault in the most offensive manner, abusing personalities and thereby quite forgetting the noble personality of Rudolf Steiner himself, who well knew what he was doing when he appointed to the members of the *Vorstand* their various functions. These attacked him in so doing, because they doubted his insight.

These three moods came clearly to light, and now it is absolutely necessary to come to an understanding with these variously disposed people, who are to be found in the Anthroposophical Society and who have expressed their opinions with these different attitudes. What was intended by the continuation of the Leading Thoughts, when Rudolf Steiner had ceased to write them down on the physical plane?

Our leader had given in the Leading Thoughts a wonderful building to the Anthroposophical Society, a building in which could be found anew, crystal-clear, the treasure of wisdom of Anthroposophy. This was given in short, pregnant sentences, in such a way that anyone at all familiar with Anthroposophy could easily understand them. The intention was that, through the study of these Leading Thoughts, which appeared regularly every week, a common link should be created between the members among themselves and between them and the *Vorstand* at the Goetheanum. When this direct and immediate activity of our leader ceased on the physical plane, we who had worked with him sought for possibilities of continuing the work. It was then that our dear Albert Steffen gave us the solution of our difficulty in these beautiful words: 'Absorb yourselves in his activity and you will find the way to Rudolf Steiner in the spiritual world.' This was also my attitude, my positive attitude. Our first task was to endeavour to retain the common activity with our spiritual leader through sinking ourselves in his work, through emphasizing and drawing attention to what had already been said, through underlining truths that had suddenly been placed in the foreground by the death of our beloved master. One could only find the way to Rudolf Steiner in the spiritual world by continually thinking over all that has been said and written by him, and by each member keeping alive within him what binds him personally with Dr Steiner. That was my way, the only way it was possible for me to tread. It was a necessity for me to bring what Dr Steiner had said to me in the course of personal conversations into harmony with what had been given and written in lectures, and to make it accessible to the members. And I place great value upon this point: only to say as much of what was entrusted to me as can also be found and verified by each member in the lectures. In this sense, the Leading Thoughts originated.

If a group of people wish to object to the chosen form they should nonetheless consider how destructively they interfere with the positive continuation of the work. A continuity in the work, extending to the form itself, should be maintained in order to avoid a division and a separation between the anthroposophical treasures of wisdom and the personality of Dr Steiner. For he himself once spoke these words: 'I have only to leave the physical plane, and if the antagonistic powers were then to succeed in separating Anthroposophy from me in such a way that the teaching would reach wide masses without any knowledge of me, so that the teaching would become shallow, then what the Ahrimanic beings have willed and purposed would actually come about.'

This utterance is to be taken in earnest and should never be forgotten, because we must also bear in mind how great the dangers are that could now arise through the increase of the Anthroposophical Society. For while the teaching may indeed spread far and wide, it may easily happen that the personality of Dr Steiner does not come to sufficient effect, unless those members who stood in a personal relation with him in earthly life are able to continue this connection now he is in the spiritual world, and thereby fulfil the duty of keeping alive his life and personality for the others.

How great the dangers are was clearly emphasized by Rudolf Steiner when he was staying in Paris, after the Christmas Foundation Meeting. In an opening lecture to members, he said that 'the Anthroposophical Movement, which now since the Christmas Foundation Meeting has been identified with the Anthroposophical Society, might become more and more esoteric, but that also connected with this was the fact that, from the spiritual side, very strong opposing powers, demonic forces, would come by storm against the Anthroposophical Society. In order to reach their object, these inimical powers make use here on Earth of those human beings who oppose the positive activity of the spiritual, whether within the Anthroposophical Society itself or working against Anthroposophy outside it.'

But at the same time Dr Steiner also expressed the hope that these opposing powers might be vanquished. And now we are faced with the burning question: have they in fact been vanquished, or could one not regard his leaving the physical plane as a deed of sacrifice in order to vanquish those demonic powers? Only much, much later will it be possible to speak about this mystery, when much that has happened stands out still more clearly. At the present time, we must receive it in reverence, uniting ourselves in love with him who did for us such mighty deeds, and uttering inwardly the prayer: O help us further, thou great spirit!

To All Members!

12 July 1925

It is with indescribable joy that I receive, from young and old, from far and near, the message: 'We will go forward in the work with courage and trust. We have confidence.' The letters that announce this are moving—there are so many forces of love, which can be transformed into forces of knowledge, and which have indeed already been so transformed. There are so many people who have the good will to share, with loving understanding, in the burden of the difficult tasks that arose for the *Vorstand* on all sides after the death of our beloved master, and thereby furnish the basis for continuing the work in the sense that Dr Steiner intended. This positive attitude is of infinite value and is what Dr Steiner considered to be the basis of anthroposophical teaching, the basis on which Anthroposophy could be built.

If one enters deeply into the Acts of the Apostles, one can read there also what enormous difficulties the disciples had to overcome after the Mystery of Golgotha. The knowledge of how bravely they struggled can be a consoling example. Every spiritual movement has to reckon with difficulties in the beginning, because each spiritual step forward in human evolution evokes opposing forces in the spiritual world which then come to life in the opposition of human beings. The negative attitude of certain individual members has shown itself to be in such a minority as no longer to need consideration. Meanwhile the positive work goes quietly on.

After the Paris Conference in May had passed off so beautifully, a conference was held in Vienna from 12 to 15 June, which Dr Wachsmuth and I attended by invitation. The Anthroposophical Society has made great progress lately in

Vienna. The Anthroposophical Society in Austria, which became fully conscious of its importance when it realized that as a spiritual movement it has great tasks to accomplish for the work in the East, has recently moved into newer and larger premises. One had the pleasant impression that here a worthy dwelling was created for the activity of Michael, for Rudolf Steiner's teachings and his exponents. A warmth of feeling radiated from the Vienna *Vorstand*. There sat the old, faithful friends, who had known Rudolf Steiner for so many years, and had gone with him from the beginning of his anthroposophical activity, standing faithfully at his side, revering and loving him, and now also ready after the death of their leader to carry on the work with rejuvenated zeal and strength, knowing well that their leader himself will not forsake them from the spiritual world. This knowledge and hope rang out in the powerful speech by Herr Breitenstein, who stirred the hearts of all present with hope for the future. In his opening address Herr Zeissig spoke words of kindness and love. Dr Lauer, in a beautifully planned lecture, showed how fully he had understood the impulse of the Christmas Foundation Meeting, and succeeded in carrying his hearers enthusiastically with him. Other interesting lectures were given and reports were made by group leaders, who all showed that work is going on in Austria, here more, there less, according to circumstances. The reports expressed very clearly the desire to have more expert speakers who could give public lectures to satisfy the need one finds everywhere among those outside the movement to hear more about Anthroposophy. The *Vorstand* of the Anthroposophical Society in Austria and the leaders of the various groups were agreed that Dr Lauer should undertake the office of travelling lecturer, so as to carry his knowledge far and wide. On behalf of the Dornach *Vorstand*, Dr Wachsmuth returned thanks for the expressions of fidelity towards it. He then spoke in inspired words about the new Goetheanum, now in process of being built, and set out the future working tasks of the individual sections of the School of Spiritual Science. In the course of the Conference, lectures were also given by Dr Schubert and Dr Kolisko, of Stuttgart, by Dr Thieben and Dr Zitkovsky, and by Dr Stein, of Stuttgart, who had to give two, one of them a public lecture entitled 'The Life and Work of Rudolf Steiner.'

In his own convincingly clear way, Dr Stein showed that one can gauge the immense importance of Rudolf Steiner's *work*, especially for our time, from his unique book *The Course of my Life*. In his life, through the union of a comprehensive knowledge of modern science with the ability to look into the spiritual worlds, there was achieved for the first time in one personality a tremendously liberating synthesis of hitherto separated currents in world history.

On Saturday we had a eurythmy demonstration, given by Fräulein Savitch and Fräulein Senft, with recitation by Fräulein Hacker. This eurythmy performance was a perfect gem. So much beauty, grace, intelligence and feeling have surely seldom been presented to the public in so impressive a manner and in such concentrated form. Response was not wanting; jubilant applause broke out with a desire for more, a craving that always arises in souls athirst for beauty. The ladies were called back several times to repeat their items. The recitation by Fräulein Hacker was likewise sympathetic and rang out distinct and clear. One felt very thankful to Frau Dr Steiner for having made possible something so beautiful.

The Conference was brought to a close, as in Paris, by a lesson for the First Class of the School of Spiritual Science, in which the fact was again brought clearly to the consciousness of the members that the Anthroposophical Society possesses treasures of wisdom, which were given to it by its master and leader, Rudolf Steiner. And it was also clearly expressed that the possession of these treasures of wisdom brings with it feelings of responsibility, for we have to try and become worthy of these gifts of wisdom, and to guard and protect them.

I also have to relate that the socializing in Vienna, at which one had opportunity to come nearer to each other on a human level, took place not only at the premises of the Society but also at the house of Herr van Leer, where a centre has been found. The kindly hostess never tired of giving full play to her hospitable nature.

We were also given the opportunity by Herr van Leer of

visiting the Burgenland by car. At certain places in that country there were ancient Danube Mystery Centres, of which Dr Steiner has also spoken in various lectures, and according to the epic it was there that Gilgamesh underwent his initiation. According to indications by Dr Steiner, in the Burgenland, on the Hungarian border, Castle Bernstein is to be found. This is also mentioned in one of Dr Steiner's Mystery Plays, and in earlier times it was a centre of Rosicrucian activity. In the neighbourhood there was said to be an antimony mine, which had existed in those days. As we had no definite information, it was a case of searching for this place, and quite a romantic search it proved to be. We had to make our way across a pathless terrain, and after a long search we at last discovered the castle in a wonderful situation, towering high up and dominating the landscape. We found a way into the castle, and were able to decipher some interesting matter from the coats of arms of the former owners, of which we will some day give a more detailed account. After long search we also located the mine, situated at some distance from the castle, and which, at the present time, is sunk in magic sleep, but, from what one could gather, is soon to be awakened from its poetical slumbers by a modern joint-stock company. When one reflects upon the important role antimony has played in earlier times for therapeutic purposes, especially through the Rosicrucian School, one can gauge how significant precisely this antimony mine was for the history of the Burgenland. There lie buried still untold treasures of ancient wisdom.

And so, with feelings of deep satisfaction and of immense gratitude to Heer van Leer, we set out on our way home. The new impulses we had received were still further heightened as we passed near Dr Steiner's home country and could let the influence of that experience work upon our hearts.

To All Members!

26 July 1925

Once more I feel impelled to say quite briefly how clearly the desire for the continuation of the Leading Thoughts has been expressed by individual branches, working groups and individual members. It has been gratifying to know that, after all, so large a number of people has understood what the intention was in carrying on the Leading Thoughts.

There was no question of wishing to step into Rudolf Steiner's place, nor of an irreverent copying of what was a great creation. The intention was rather to take firm hold of what was necessary in the difficult times. Countless letters and remarks have testified to the need of holding fast that spiritual bond created among the members within the Anthroposophical Society by Rudolf Steiner's Leading Thoughts. The continuity of the work could not be preserved by the repetition of the existing Leading Thoughts. These classical sentences of instruction, comprising in such a marvellous way the whole teaching of Anthroposophy, should stand as a whole; they are a wonderful study material accessible to everyone. By continuity, I mean that the living word should sound again from man to man through the Newssheet. Not that just any word one pleased might be spoken, but that one should draw from the treasures of wisdom that Rudolf Steiner has left to us, in order to bring into the foreground and to illuminate now this, now that, according to what is important for the changed conditions of the times. The changed conditions arise from the fact that the store of wisdom, which our leader had brought to us regularly in such abundance from the spiritual world, is for the time being shut away from us, and that further work can only consist in bringing forward, from out of the treasures of wisdom, certain facts that are of importance for the present moment. In the lectures and articles much lies hidden, much that was spoken long ago, but which could only later in given circumstances be rightly understood and come into men's consciousness.

This active going forward is what was intended in the continuation of the Leading Thoughts. It was felt that the bond between the members must not be allowed to grow slack and that we should always have a feeling of what binds us together.

When the saddest of all sad events had taken place, when our beloved leader left us on the physical plane, I became strongly conscious of the fact that we now find ourselves under the rulership of Michael. And then arose in me the memory of all that I had been permitted to experience, that was connected with Michael, that I had been allowed to hear from the lectures, as well as from the many utterances of Rudolf Steiner and conversations with him that it had been my privilege, my karma, to have. I became clearly conscious of the extraordinary importance Rudolf Steiner has ascribed to the dawn of Michael's rulership, how through the events connected with the Christmas Meeting and through active living deed he has brought the rulership of Michael to full and complete expression. And so the impulse ripened in me to emphasize this activity of Michael through articles and Leading Thoughts in the News-sheet.

In my previous article, I spoke of how in the course of various lectures Rudolf Steiner conjured up before our souls in tremendous pictures the preceding epoch of Michael's rulership, which lasted approximately from the year 601 until 247 BC. The activity of Aristotle with that of his pupil Alexander the Great was described; it was shown how Alexander the Great was taught to penetrate into the natural-scientific work of Aristotle, into which had flowed, through the influence of Plato, the Eleusinian Mystery Wisdom. Esoteric instructions were given to him by Aristotle, in whom lived so vividly the Ephesian Mysteries, which taught the secrets of the Word. The young Alexander was also led to Samothrace, where, with Aristotle, he also visited the Mystery

School and there received instruction. The Michael Impulse worked so strongly in him that he felt within himself the urge to *experience* what he had been taught and to carry out into the world the knowledge imparted to him by Aristotle.

When the Michael Impulse lives in earthly humanity, then what in the beginning was taught in a spiritual centre is carried further over many peoples of the Earth and spread far and wide in all regions where there exist possibilities of spiritual activity. Thus originated the campaigns of Alexander, through which also the whole of Aristotelian knowledge was brought to the East, esoterically and exoterically. Here one can speak of a *Michael Stream*.

But something else also happens during this rulership of Michael. Somewhat earlier than the campaigns of Alexander, those of the Arthurian knights took place, going out from the west coast of England. Twelve knights gathered together at King Arthur's Round Table, learned Michael-warriors who, coming from the West, had the task of civilizing Central and Northern Europe, and of liberating the people who dwelt there from their wild astrality, which they exorcised out of themselves in the shape of wild animals. These Arthurian knights had the faculty enabling them to behold the impulses that came from the Sun, where the great Christ-Being still had his dwelling, in the play of Nature, in which, as Rudolf Steiner said, the Sun-born spirits meet the Earth-born spirits; they could behold them in the water or in the air, and receive them in their own ethereal bodies. With this force of the Sun-Christ within them they were able to take up the fight against the astral beasts, to conquer them and to purify those regions and peoples, in order to prepare them for the reception of the Sun Impulse.

Here also it is possible to speak of a Michael Stream, which proceeds from *West to East*. And this current was continued, after the period of the rulership of Michael had expired, in a Christian Stream, in which the Christ was still experienced in Nature, even after He had already come down to the Earth.

The other Michael Stream, which started with Alexander, spread from Asia over North Africa as far as Spain and found an outlet in Ireland, in the Hibernian Mysteries—a current

that went from *East to West*. This current later continued into
the Grail Stream, after the Mystery of Golgotha had taken
place, and met in Europe with the Arthurian Stream.

Now what do these Streams signify? It is important that we
who are again living in a Michael Age should clearly apprehend
these Streams. And the question arises, which direction will
the Streams take in our Michael Age? What has the will to
arise, now that we find ourselves in the dawn of Michael's
rulership? The spiritual—the anthroposophical wisdom that
was taught, as we know, in supersensible worlds by Michael—
has concentrated itself in one definite point in Central Europe,
in Dornach. And the Michael Impulse, rightly understood,
works in a cosmopolitan way. So the task for us, who stand
under the Michael Impulse, will be to spread further the
treasures of wisdom, letting them radiate out everywhere.
Michael's chief direction, and especially in the future, will be
towards the *North-East*. And united with Michael will go those
individualities who had formerly also worked in the Aristotle-
Alexander Stream and in the Arthurian Stream.

When one considers what undermining forces are pressing
forward from the East towards the West and are even now
manifest in the most recent world events, one can appreciate
what a tremendous significance the direction North-East will
have, and what a great and special responsibility those centres
have that are already established in the East, and from which
Anthroposophy is being carried forward like a wall of light
towards the East. Indeed, in the last period of his life Rudolf
Steiner often warned us that we are standing on a volcano
which may erupt at any moment, unless sufficient spiritual
force is present on Earth to prevent this. And sufficient
spiritual force will be there, if all that streams into our age
through Michael can be brought into action.

Leading Thoughts

In the earlier Michael Age, which lasted from about the year
601 to 247 BC, there were Michael Streams flowing from East
to West, and continuing again from West to Eastern and

Northern Europe.

In the present Michael Age there is a spiritual centre in Middle Europe, with the Michael Impulse to spread out in a cosmopolitan, radiating way. The main direction that Michael takes is North-East, and will principally be so in the future as well.

Out of the former Michael Streams many souls meet again today in the present Michael Age. They come to Anthroposophy and have the will to become conscious of how Michael works in Anthroposophy.

To All Members!

2 August 1925

We are now living in the Michael Age, and in order to be able fully to understand Michael's activity we will bring together all the building stones given us by Rudolf Steiner. He gave them to us in order to waken us out of the sleep in which we now find ourselves, to show us the *tasks* incumbent upon us. It will have to become ever clearer to us how deeply we are united with Michael, and that Anthroposophy is a Michael Impulse, which was deepened, illuminated from all sides, brought out from the spiritual world and made comprehensible on Earth for humanity in its present state of consciousness by Rudolf Steiner.

We heard that Michael is concerned with the development of the cosmic intelligence; that he, as the most important Archangel and Sun Spirit, had to renounce his rulership of the cosmic intelligence as a result of the natural development of the world order, and how this cosmic intelligence came to Earth and became the property of mankind. In the earlier period of his rulership, Michael sent down intellectuality with the physical Sun-rays, and the men who were receptive to it were inspired by this cosmic intellectuality. These Inspirations took place in the old Sun Mysteries, where these secrets were known.

Gradually the time came when men developed intellectuality in themselves, through their own power. By the eighth century AD this process was completed, and we find people on Earth with thoughts of their own, which was not yet to any extent possible *before* the complete descent of cosmic intelligence. This time was prepared through the philosophy of Aristotle, in which was expressed the slow releasing of the

earthly intellect from cosmic intellectuality. And this was also
the time wherein the Mystery Centres gradually vanished.

The necessity for the cosmic intelligence to be given over to
the world lay in the fact that the Christ-Being united himself
with the Earth. With the descent of the Christ the sign was
given for Michael to give up the rulership of this cosmic
intelligence. But in doing so Michael was placed in the
strange position of no longer being able to send his Impulses
down on to the Earth. He had to wait until his own period of
rulership dawned once more, which happened only in 1879,
while earlier he had the power even outside these periods of
giving out his Impulses continually from the Sun. By renoun-
cing his rulership over the cosmic intelligence, Michael had
come to a state of inactivity.

On Earth, people were now without any impulse from
Michael; this was most noticeable from the fifteenth century
onwards, when the consciousness soul began to develop in
mankind. Human beings had certainly their own thoughts,
but no impulses from the spiritual world could be given to
them.

In this period, Michael sought to renew the bond with
mankind by gathering round him from the fifteenth to the
seventeenth and eighteenth centuries souls who found themselves in the spiritual world and who had been united with
him in the previous Michael Age. Here he could gather round
him the leading individuals of the time when the Dominicans
were in their prime, and the souls connected with them—the
souls from the time of Alexander and the souls of the
Platonists who had worked in the School of Chartres. To
these were added a large number of striving and seeking souls
who united with them. Michael assembled all these round
him, and instructed them. Thereby arose a supersensible
School, in which was taught all that had been proclaimed in
the Mystery Centres as initiation wisdom in ancient and
primeval times. The souls took part in something extraordinary that happened for the first time in the spiritual world
under Michael's leadership; and what these souls then experienced impressed itself deeply upon them.

Before this time, the karma of the following earth life had

been prepared and worked out by the human souls under the guidance of spiritual beings during the period between death and a new birth. But *in the particular way* in which it was taught in this supersensible school, karma had never before been fashioned, so the souls had never yet received enlightenment about the laws of karma. And when they again returned to the Earth, the souls prepared in this way felt an impulse to unite themselves with the Anthroposophical Movement. In this Movement they found—in their at first unconscious impulse—the continuation of what they had experienced in the supersensible before their life on Earth. Deep in their hearts—inwardly bound up with their karma—rested the knowledge given to them by Michael.

To occupy oneself now in Anthroposophy with the laws of karma means to occupy oneself with the teachings of Michael, which have been given in the spiritual world.

An earthly polar antithesis to the activity of Michael is the work of Ahriman, who from the Earth tries to destroy what Michael imparts as wisdom teaching. Ahriman works ceaselessly here in opposition to Michael, and human beings, left to themselves—without inspiration from Michael—are in constant danger of falling into Ahriman's clutches. And now, at the dawn of the Michael Age, Anthroposophy is confronted by this danger. Its task is to lead men to the experiencing of what was taught by Michael in the fifteenth, sixteenth and seventeenth centuries and what was given by Michael in the form of tremendous pictures right on into the nineteenth century, in order to awaken man to a higher state of consciousness.

But just in this heightened consciousness Ahriman sees the greatest danger to the development of his power. It suits him well to keep men in a sleeping condition, because then the effects of karma are not experienced consciously. He opposes with all his power the revelations of the laws of karma. Watchfulness and conscious experience in man are very disagreeable to Ahriman, because he can only exert his influence on those who *do not have* this watchful consciousness.

In the present period of Michael's rulership, the further

development of mankind demands the revelation of the laws of karma. This is also demanded by the further development of the Anthroposophical Movement and of the souls connected with it.

If the recognition of karma is suppressed by Ahriman—and this comes to expression in people in the fear they have of concerning themselves with it—then the Michael Impulses will be lost, and the first century of our Michael Age will pass away without the occurrence of what should have taken place as the task entrusted by Michael to his faithful ones. But then human civilization will follow the path to the abyss and will not find the path of light appointed by the Gods.

But there is also another greatly threatening danger, coming from a different direction, from the side of Lucifer. If the necessary earnestness does not reign in the hearts of men, if humility and good will do not enter into the souls of those who occupy themselves with these tremendous truths, then Lucifer gains power over these souls. Ahriman does not want the laws of karma to be experienced consciously in the hearts of men; Lucifer rejoices when men take up problems of karma in a frivolous, self-sufficient and self-important spirit. Those human beings who have received Anthroposophy into themselves in the right way will go between Ahriman and Lucifer, and will unerringly follow Michael, who goes ahead, sure of his goal, pointing out the way. The dangers which threaten from the right, through the whisperings of Ahriman, and the dangers which threaten from the left, through the enticements of Lucifer, these we must recognize courageously, fully aware of the presence of Ahriman and Lucifer, but not allowing ourselves to be led astray by them, going forward, in order to carry into action the Impulse of Michael.

Leading Thoughts

Karma revelations are necessary in the present Michael Age, for the development of mankind demands this.

Ahriman opposes the revelations of karma, because the knowledge of karma destroys his power. Lucifer takes possession of those souls who in a frivolous way, without firm foundation, occupy themselves with the question of karma.

The Michael Impulse requires a heightened waking-consciousness, in order to recognize the workings of Ahriman and Lucifer. A selfless study of karmic relationships means a sure overcoming of Ahriman and Lucifer, and signifies the victory of Michael.

To All Members!

9 August 1925

In explaining the karma of the Anthroposophical Society, Dr Steiner has spoken about two groups of people to be found in it.

Whoever can observe human beings will be well able to distinguish and assess the kind of personality that belongs to each of these two groups.

One group of souls consists of those who, as active anthroposophists with strong will impulses, are endeavouring to take into themselves all that Anthroposophy can give. Principally it is the teaching of cosmology in Anthroposophy to which they feel themselves attracted. They possess great understanding for the Cosmic Christ, but in finding the way to Anthroposophy they have sought not so much the Christ as a world-embracing view of life. And within the Anthroposophical Movement these souls are endeavouring to spread these teachings further among men. These are souls who have gone through their most important and significant incarnation in the pre-Christian era. They were steeped in heathenism, were closely connected with the wisdom of the mysteries, and many of them could look into the spiritual world. They were souls who had not had many earth incarnations but had undergone their development chiefly on the planets rather than on the Earth, and only gradually after the Atlantean period did they incarnate again on the Earth. Therefore they still had a certain freshness, rather than earthly weariness, and also still had possibilities to look into the spiritual world.

These souls, who had their decisive incarnations in the pre-

Christian era, did not go through the first centuries of
Christianity; during the Mystery of Golgotha and in the
time immediately following they found themselves in the
spiritual world. They underwent their next important incarnation only after the seventh and eighth centuries, and there
they embraced Christianity. But besides Christology they still
also kept their heathen knowledge, which still worked powerfully on in them, and which they found more or less mixed
with Christianity, for Christianity had not yet worked itself
completely free from paganism. They pondered much over
Christianity, and were connected with it more through their
intellect than their feelings. In these souls there lived the
Aristotelian impulse and there also lived strongly the Michael
Impulses of the then period of Michael's rulership.

Another group of men may be found within the Anthroposophical Society. It consists of those souls of a more
contemplative nature who in their present incarnation have
a great leaning towards Anthroposophy but who do not feel
the need to be active within the Anthroposophical Movement.
They have a great yearning to find the Christ and are greatly
satisfied if Anthroposophy can lead them to the Christ-Being,
for whom in the depths of their soul life there lives a warm,
longing feeling. For the cosmic teachings of Anthroposophy
they have no special inclination and are more or less indiffer-
ent towards them. In the existing theological knowledge they
find nothing to satisfy the desire for the Christ that they carry
in their subconsciousness. They feel themselves drawn to
Anthroposophy directly they hear of its teachings.

These souls have gone through many earthly incarnations
as far back as the Atlantean epoch. In their pre-Christian
incarnations they had, in the then existing Sun Oracle,
reverenced the Christ-Being as found in the Sun, with an
instinctive clairvoyant consciousness, which they afterwards
gradually lost. And when these souls again returned to Earth
at the time of the Mystery of Golgotha and in the early
Christian centuries, they possessed no more a clairvoyant
knowledge of the Sun-Being but only a more or less living
tradition. Gradually this tradition, too, became more and
more lost, and of the Mystery of Golgotha many just had

only the conception that a God from somewhere had joined himself to a human body and as Jesus of Nazareth had walked the Earth. No longer conscious that this God was a Sun God, they began to argue about the matter in Church Councils and finally accepted what was dictated from Rome. But some of these souls, who still retained as living memory the tradition that the Christ was a Sun-Being, could not be influenced by these Councils, and because they persisted in their belief they were called heretics, as also were many souls who belong to the first group and bear within themselves the knowledge of the Sun-Christ. The souls just described had their decisive incarnations in the first century of our era, during or soon after the Mystery of Golgotha. And in their incarnations of the pre-Christian period they had taken into themselves much Platonism.

Now before these two groups of souls incarnated again at the present time, they both together received those mighty Imaginations that at the beginning of the nineteenth century were given by Michael in the supersensible world.

The group of souls who underwent their decisive incarnations in the pre-Christian era knew that Christ had come down from the Sun to the Earth, for during the time of the Mystery of Golgotha they themselves had witnessed in the supersensible worlds the departure of the Christ-Being from the Sun and had understood this event through their mystery-knowledge. This group, when they received the mighty Imaginations presented to them by Michael— Imaginations that revealed in pictures the whole cosmology and the secrets of the Christ-Being—received the strongest impulses to become really true Christians when they came again to the Earth, such Christians as would have a strong will to carry down all that was there in those mighty pictures and to transform it for the Earth so that mankind could understand.

The other group of souls, who had their decisive incarnation in the first centuries after Christ, and who still experienced the Mystery of Golgotha or were still strongly impressed by it, did not recognize Christ as the Sun God any more. These souls fell into complete uncertainty when later, in the time between death and a new birth, they did not find Christ in the Sun. They did not receive the supersensible Imaginations in so wide-awake a state of soul as the first group, so that when they came to the Earth, though they had indeed, through a subconscious memory of what had been experienced in the supersensible worlds, the longing and the impulse to find Christ on the Earth, yet they were not stirred to the point of activity. They have a strong leaning towards Anthroposophy without the wish to be active in it.

It is important, says Dr Steiner, to find out to which of these groups one belongs, to examine oneself so that as an anthroposophist one gains a feeling of belonging to one or other of these groups.

Why is this so important? Since the Anthroposophical Movement has a mission to fulfil that consists in bringing the treasure of wisdom to mankind, it is necessary that the persons who are actively working in it should have this knowledge about themselves. The way in which each will work will be different according to the group to which he belongs. Those men who had their decisive incarnation in pre-Christian times will make the best progress and will find their way back into the spiritual world, if they chiefly concern themselves with a deepening of cosmological relationships. Their meditational work goes in this direction. Those who experienced their decisive incarnations in the first centuries after Christ develop their finest powers by entering deeply into Christianity as illuminated by Anthroposophy, and by carrying the new Christianity into the future.

The recognition of both these types of men is of great importance too in the new art of healing. In dealing with illness, the doctor will try to heal the type of persons first described by way of the head system and metabolic system; in the second group, on the contrary, the healing forces must be stimulated through the rhythmic system. Of course, there are those who come between these two groups, and the doctor especially has plenty of opportunity to observe them. For working oneself deeply into the art of healing means also an intensive effort to come to know the human being, and this again is closely connected to people's karma.

Leading Thoughts

In the Anthroposophical Society two principal groups of souls may be found, and it is necessary for the future and mission of the Anthroposophical Movement that each individual should recognize to which of these groups he belongs.

One of these groups had its decisive incarnations in pre-Christian times. To it belong those souls who found their way to Anthroposophy through their urge to acquire a knowledge of cosmological connections. They have in them the impulse to activity.

The other group had their decisive incarnations at the time of the Mystery of Golgotha and in the first Christian centuries. The souls belonging to it seek for a deepened Christianity within the Anthroposophical Movement. They are the more contemplative natures who bring their warmth of heart towards the Christ.

Between these groups there are also souls who have affinity with one or other of these types, but are not so firmly rooted as them in the Anthroposophical Movement.

To All Members!

16 August 1925

As so much unclarity seems to prevail concerning the institution of the three classes of the School of Spiritual Science at the Goetheanum it is necessary to say something about it here.

What was intended with the institution of the three classes of the School of Spiritual Science? The longing of the members of the Anthroposophical Society to enter into the esoteric was to be fulfilled by this School. This had become possible when the intentions that underlay the Christmas Foundation Meeting were carried into effect.

In Anthroposophy the truths of the spiritual world are conveyed to us in the form of ideas that require no more than rationality and objective judgement in the seeker and can be taken hold of through purely objective thinking. And it is in this way that spiritual science is cultivated in the General Anthroposophical Society. The esoteric, on the other hand, is that wealth of teaching that reveals itself to the seer in the form of Imaginations, Inspirations and Intuitions and communicated, in a language that men can understand, to those who do not wish to restrict themselves to taking up the spiritual world in the form of ideas alone. And it was for such people within the Anthroposophical Society who seek the direct way into the spiritual world that the institution of the three classes was intended. So on 15 February 1924 Dr Steiner began with the establishment of the First Class, at first with a small number of people, who were mostly living in Dornach itself.

The precondition for being received into this First Class was a two years' intensive study of Anthroposophy which had led to a thorough familiarity with this treasure of wisdom.

Together with this should be the ability to represent Anthroposophy rationally but also with one's whole being. For the present age requires a conscious placing of oneself into the spiritual world, so that a wide-awake consciousness is necessary for the longing to find the way into the spiritual worlds.

So it was Dr Steiner's wish that those individuals who, after examining themselves, had resolved to apply for the First Class should be personally known to himself or to members of the *Vorstand*. When this was not the case it was necessary to await the opportunity for such a personal acquaintance. This, too, is the reason why many who have applied have not yet been admitted.

After the Christmas Foundation Meeting the various sections at the Goetheanum were also established. Thus the sciences, such as medicine, natural science and astronomy, and the arts, such as recitation, eurythmy, music and poetry, received their own centres within the School. And the sciences and arts, which are cultivated in their several sections, will have the possibility of being deepened by the results of spiritual knowledge, so that from the School, as Dr Steiner intended, the work in the sections may be made fruitful, illumined and inspired.

At that time our teacher intended to institute Class Lessons, personally at first, in various other German centres and national Societies. In several national Societies it was also possible to fulfil this intention, though unfortunately not in Germany.

The urgent question is now: how shall this First Class of the School be further carried on, since Rudolf Steiner is no longer on the physical plane? It is more and more apparent how exceedingly great the longing is for the esoteric. Applications for membership of the First Class increase day by day, so that the number of members is already very considerable.

Shortly before his illness, Dr Steiner had resolved to establish the Second and Third Classes of the School. Had this taken place, the overfilling of the First Class, by which the intimacy necessary for esoteric teachings might be lost, would naturally have been avoided.

Unfortunately this plan was not carried through, and only

the communications of the First Class remain. And it is now our duty to guard this content and carry it forward in the right way. It is our endeavour to expand and bring to human understanding, even as it is bequeathed to us, this School that is connected to Michael and is a continuation of his supersensible instructions. Therefore one of the first rulings should be that the members of the Class are enabled to receive the several Class Lessons in regular succession. It is utterly wrong, for instance, that a newly admitted member has to start with the middle or even the last lesson without having received the first ones. To begin with such a procedure was admittedly unavoidable, but if one were to continue in this way one would not after all attain what can be attained, namely, that one should find the way to the spiritual world and become familiar with it.

The School could be carried on in the best way if each one received at regular intervals what belongs to its continuous instructions, and so the number of those partaking in the single lessons would not be too great and the intimate character of the lessons thus remain preserved. If the School can be successfully expanded in this way, then something great will be attained, because Michael's words will everywhere resound, with his Will working in every properly disposed pupil of the School. For England, this has already been successfully carried out, and it is to be hoped that this work may be continued in other countries as well.

To All Members!

20 September 1925

Michael-thoughts, those that move us deeply now, are working in our souls, reminding us of the events that took place and moved us so deeply a year ago. Rudolf Steiner, our so infinitely honoured and beloved teacher, our leader and true friend, withdrew on 29 September from his outer activities, after we had been addressed with words so full of meaning on the Michaelmas Day of the preceding year. A bodily exhaustion overcame him, which at length he could no longer master, and which then unceasingly consumed his already weakened reserve forces, with which till then he had worked so economically. And so we had also to experience how his physical forces became weaker and weaker, while the spirit in him revealed itself the more radiantly and mightily. For to that period we owe all those significant communications about Michael. During that time we were introduced to an understanding of the working and the mission of Michael. It was what Rudolf Steiner had wanted to give us after the Christmas Foundation Meeting, joined at the same time with the active deeds of Michael. He had intended to make Michael festivals live in the manner of the mysteries, so that they should not be experienced instinctively as in earlier times, but in the form suited to our present Age of the Consciousness Soul.

Unhappily this work could no longer be accomplished, and shortly before Easter this wonderful man left the physical plane, he who had given to mankind things of such indescribable value, which perhaps will only be understood in their full greatness and importance in subsequent generations by a larger number than those who are now inside the Anthroposophical Society. He left behind a number of human beings, a number of souls truly devoted to him, loving him and striving to understand him.

At first we could not grasp it. Only slowly does understanding find its way into the soul thirsting for knowledge, and comfort is given to it. What are the Michael-thoughts that are so helpful and effective?

We will now once more briefly remember all that Rudolf Steiner told us about Michael and Michael's activity in the course of human evolution, how Michael prepared for his Earth mission, which falls within the age of evolution of the consciousness soul. Michael guides the descent of the cosmic intelligence, for he himself is connected with this cosmic intelligence. And after the necessity has arisen for mankind in its further evolution to come to this intellectuality, he resolves to remain with intellectuality, to take the way from the cosmos to the human being. He has been on this way since the eighth century AD, and it was only in the last third of the nineteenth century that he reached his earthly activity. From that time onwards Michael is to be found in the region of the supersensible world that directly adjoins our physical world of sense, and is only severed from the visible world by a thin veil—in the ethereal world, in the world of living thoughts. Here the man of today who lives in living thoughts will be able to find Michael, who, inspiring mankind, can work as a real force among them. He shows himself in a radiant aura of light with warning gesture or with flashing sword.

Michael was ever the great inspirer of mankind. And formerly, when the ego and astral body were less firmly united with the physical-ethereal organism, spiritual beings could then reveal themselves as thoughts within the ego. Great deeds were accomplished as expressions of the divine beings standing behind mankind. In this way Michael, too, had been able to work.

Later on, when human evolution had gone further, the divine beings could then no longer make themselves known in this way, and it was the *reflection* of these beings that was now revealed in the soul life of mankind. Ever more and more the connection with the spiritual world was lost, which was necessary for the evolution of the consciousness soul. And as the consciousness soul evolved more and more in man, complete separation from the spiritual world was also taking place. Thoughts could henceforth be experienced only in the physical body, as the dead shadows of the spiritual.

Here the possibility is given to man to come to his very own will and thus to attain to freedom. But with this the danger of falling a victim to the power of Ahriman, whose sphere of influence is the Earth, has become that much greater. Man, on the other hand, when he had lived in direct union with the spiritual world, was protected by the Gods of the Hierarchies against Ahriman. This protection had continued up to the dawn of the Age of the Consciousness Soul.

As this present-day thinking is firmly united with the earthly body, Michael unfortunately cannot approach it. Filled with anxiety, he sees how mankind comes more and more under the influence of Ahriman, and he looks for ways to approach human beings. His task is by his own power to revivify and set free the ethereal bodies of men, which have been fettered by the hardening forces of the physical. Then man will be able to attain to living thoughts again, and will be capable of receiving the divine Inspirations.

It is a deep tragedy that, despite all the efforts of Michael and despite the search of significant personalities in our age for the human being within themselves, the inspiring voice of Michael is generally not heard. Satisfaction with the knowledge of nature, which has taken hold of man and altogether captivated him, is the greatest hindrance to this. And though significant ideas were evolved by exceptional men in the present Age of the Consciousness Soul in the most varied realms of spiritual life, and though these ideas sought for the full experience of man, they could not lead to an experience of the realm of Michael. In art Michael forces still broke through here and there, for instance during the Renaissance time in Raphael, and later in the poetic art of Novalis. But these forces were no longer able to send their light into the consciousness soul. With ever-increasing anxiety Michael witnessed the activities of men. It became urgent to find a solution.

And this solution Rudolf Steiner brought. He heard the

Inspiration that came from the deep anxiety of Michael somewhat as follows: 'Will men in their illusion give so much power to Ahriman, to the Dragon, that it will be impossible for him, Michael, to help them in the right manner? And the right manner of his help consists in this, that he would bring man again as in former times into connection with the Gods without that Luciferic element which also seeks to bind man to the Gods, but severed from the Earth. Michael, too, though keeping him united with the Earth, would give man so much spirituality that he can remain free from Ahriman.' A further question of the Inspiration was: 'Can this balance really be maintained by him, Michael?'

Rudolf Steiner received the Inspiration, and a wonderful thing took place in that, for the first time in the fully evolved consciousness soul of a human being within this Age of the Consciousness Soul, the otherwise dead thoughts became alive again. The thoughts rose to life in the ether body, and it was possible to write the book *The Philosophy of Freedom*, which became a book of Michael. Rudolf Steiner, as he himself stated, experienced from the year 1889 to the year 1896 the world of the ethereal adjoining the world of the senses. There he experienced the ethereal world of thought.

Thus the Michael Mission in the present age could first reveal itself in Rudolf Steiner. In him there first arose thoughts kindled to life and of such potency that souls and spirits of the supersensible world inclined to these enlivened thoughts. He was the man made free, who could live with the spiritual beings as once upon a time the human being in the mysteries had lived with them.

Thus there began the mystery that continued throughout the life and work of Rudolf Steiner until the time of his sickness. Not only Michael expressed himself through him, even far higher powers made themselves known; Michael became the servant of his spirit.

A beginning had been made. The consciousness soul of a human being, for whom through his former incarnations it was possible to reach into the spiritual world, was so kindled to life by the power of Michael that his entry into the spiritual world could become a reality.

With this real grasp of the spiritual world the boundaries of natural science had been broken through, and it was made possible for man to recognize on a purely epistemological path the world that lives behind the world of sense. Natural science, however, represented by men whose consciousness souls still held fast to dead thoughts, could not yet bring any understanding towards this way of experience of Rudolf Steiner. Among these men he found at first the gates still closed. But a group of men was found who, from a deep sympathy of feeling, had some understanding for such spiritual knowledge. Through this understanding Anthroposophy was bestowed on them by Rudolf Steiner. It was a matter of course that these men came to Rudolf Steiner, for the old Rosicrucianism was still living in their souls. For it had been the case that Michael forces had worked in the Rosicrucians even into the Middle Ages, where Michael had found in them the men whom he could still approach. For the Rosicrucians in earlier times were among the last to have a still living connection with the spiritual world when the transition took place to the Age of the Consciousness Soul. And many of those who came to Anthroposophy were souls who had been united with this Rosicrucianism in their former lives.

So by working with this anthroposophical treasure of wisdom, the imaginative conceptions could enter again into the souls of men, taking the place of the abstract knowledge of nature. With this, Michael was again given the possibility of approaching human beings.

And if one realizes how easily now people who are in the period of their life when their intellectual and sentient soul is evolving, and who enthusiastically concern themselves with Anthroposophy, can gain an experience of the ethereal world, where they can meet Michael and let themselves be inspired by him, then one will be aware of what an enormous task Anthroposophy has to fulfil: to bring this to the seekers who wish to experience their humanity. And an immense thankfulness arises in our souls, that there has been a man who lived among us and was with us and could bestow such a living treasure of wisdom on mankind.

Leading Thoughts

Michael, who had to fulfil his earthly mission in the age when the consciousness soul was evolving, was in deep anxiety lest he should not be able to approach human beings, because they were excessively inclined to the earthly.

Progress in the evolution of mankind could only become possible if Inspirations were received from Michael into the consciousness souls of human beings.

Through Rudolf Steiner's *Philosophy of Freedom*, in which the strength of Michael holds sway, humanity can rise again to living thoughts and thus reach an experience of the spirit. Anthroposophy is the further gift through which imaginative conceptions can again enter the consciousness souls of mankind, and it becomes possible again to receive the Inspirations of Michael.

To All Members!

4 October 1925

Michael's day is drawing near.

Our heart is moved with pain; every day brings back memories that unite us deeply with our beloved teacher, Rudolf Steiner. A year ago, at this very time, shortly before Michaelmas, dark clouds of anxiety were gathering together.

The last lectures of the courses being given in September to the various Sections, and to the priests of the Christian Community, were over. Summoning up all his forces, to many still seemingly inexhaustible, he had given to the very last, and few recognized that with these exertions the physical body was spending its final resources of strength. One observed indeed that his features became weary, his walk was often heavy and limp. But who thought of a breakdown?

Yet those who found themselves in Rudolf Steiner's immediate surroundings had to experience immeasurable pain, since at close quarters one saw the danger of a breakdown coming. Particularly observing as a doctor, one constantly asked oneself whether the coming day would bring with it an improvement or a further diminution of strength.

After the event many may ask: 'Were all those lectures and courses, which were given right to the end, a necessity? Would it not have been wiser to take more of a rest after the journey to Torquay and London, which had still taken place shortly before?'

A philistine thinking could only think in this way. In the spirit there was another point of view. 'These lectures do not tire me at all,' said Rudolf Steiner, when he was begged to take things easy. 'It is these lectures that keep me in good health,' he said. 'What is tiring are the dead thoughts that approach one; it is the incomprehension, the non-understanding of people that leaves one maimed.'

And there was a still deeper reason why these tremendous exertions were made during the Michaelmas season of last year. It was as though Rudolf Steiner wanted to make every effort to attain spiritually something of what was to be attained. It was also as though he would protect himself and ward away influences of illness. And one could see with one's own eyes how the body, at the beginning of a lecture often still so tired, grew more and more fresh during the lecture, and at last stood before us seemingly strong and rejuvenated. Every time one could share in this metamorphosis proceeding from the spirit—that was his therapy.

Often in those days I felt an infinite depression, and I could not rid my thoughts of a communication that Rudolf Steiner himself had given me some time after the Christmas Foundation Meeting.

It is certainly time today to speak again about these things, and it would not be right to withhold important matters that were told by our teacher. For we live in hard times and it is now high time to have knowledge of spiritual happenings.

One day, Rudolf Steiner told me how mercilessly the anti-Michael demons were setting to work to prevent the rise of Michael and to destroy his work. They conceal such intentions, and only human beings are able to unlock their secrets from the demons. It is only human beings who can have knowledge of demons' secrets. The Gods wait for these secrets, which men bring to them, and it is the Gods who in turn can only solve for mankind the riddle of these secrets of the demons. When human beings thus offer up to the Gods the secrets that they wrest from the demons, the sinister activity of these demons is averted, so that where darkness has held sway the spiritual light can shine again.

These anti-Michael demons, to whom also Klingsor and his hosts belong, were hard at work and threatened derisively to come into their own if the Michael Impulses that had begun so strongly should not be able to break through.

My anxious question was: what will happen if this does not succeed? And the answer was: then karma will hold sway.

The worries that were called forth by such communications weighed heavily, and it became still more difficult for me when, on Michael's day, the *last* lecture was given and Rudolf Steiner had to lie down upon his sick bed.

And so, inexorably, karma held further sway. We all know how painfully events further unfolded. Karma required the sacrifice of death. And so we stand before a deep mystery, the full implications of which it would certainly be presumptuous to wish to explain. Deep earnestness must come upon us all when we ponder and try to find out so as to have the will to grasp what then happened. And there stirs in our heart, at first gently, then becoming ever clearer and more powerful, the impulse to atone for this sacrificial death, to hold ourselves ready and open for the spiritual help that from now onward is seeking to pour down with real power.

Alas if there are no open hearts to receive it and let it work through them! Then demons will be able to prolong their evil work. And the darkness that was lit up through the sacrifice might again be darkened.

To let such earnest thoughts pass through one's soul is fitting at this time for the earnest pupils and servants of Michael, to become clear how critical the situation is in this time, and how great the catastrophe would be if Michael's willing and working could not come to its full breakthrough for the salvation of mankind. With all the activity that has lived and expressed itself so hopefully during these days, such thoughts and memories are also necessary, admonishing one to inner reflection and leading anew to strong impulses. Thus also the responsibility for the work and the continued working of Rudolf Steiner is strongly reawakened in us, and we feel ourselves united in strong will, joined together as hosts of service in the light of Michael, in the love of the Gods, in Time and Eternity.

To All Members!
On the occasion of the Youth Conference

11 October 1925

For the second time this year the young people have held a Conference at Dornach. On such an occasion it is important that we should call to mind what Rudolf Steiner himself said about young persons and the Youth Movement. He spoke about this many times, sometimes from one aspect and sometimes from another. But it was always in such a way that took the young *seriously*.

He, a man of 64 years, had an all-embracing understanding for the seeking of the young. Anyone who as a young person had the good fortune to have spoken to him will preserve this inextinguishably in his memory, for it is certain that no other man will have understood him with such warmth and depth of feeling.

It was a moment of utmost importance when one day a group of young people found themselves together in the Anthroposophical Society, carrying with them all the thoughts and feelings that the young human being of today has within him, in the expectation of finding in Anthroposophy his true humanity.

Rudolf Steiner described the event as a karmic meeting. He explained that the souls born in the present age, after the end of Kali Yuga, took part in tremendous cosmic experiences in the spiritual world before their descent to Earth. These souls, he said, really witnessed a movement in regions above the Earth, a movement of immense significance taking place behind the scenes of physical existence. It was that movement which in the Anthroposophical Society has been called the Michael Movement. Within the spiritual guidance of man-

kind there is in this Michael Movement the striving to bring
about in mankind a new development of the soul forces. And
the constitution of soul that was predominant till the end of
the nineteenth century has to give place to a new constitution
of soul that must be unfolded in the twentieth century. With
the dominion of Michael, the death of the old civilization is
also approaching.

Young people carry with them a powerful though unconscious feeling of all that they have experienced in the supersensible. Hence their dissatisfaction with existing institutions,
their inability to find their way into the requirements of an
outlived civilization, and their longing for something new that
has never been before. This longing can often lead to illness,
and drives the young souls into lonely isolation when they are
deeply disappointed not to have found what they are seeking
for, namely, the human being with the new constitution of
soul. The stronger among these young souls wrestle their way
through from this subconscious feeling to a clearer grasp of
what it is that they are feeling and can thus approach Anthroposophy, which then takes on karmic significance for them.
For as we know through Rudolf Steiner, it is Anthroposophy
that is revealed to us from the Michael Movement.

If we let work on us the things that Rudolf Steiner said
about them, we cannot but regard the young with altogether
different eyes than is otherwise done. We feel the deep
responsibility that rests on us, as human beings, to understand these young people. Those, too, who are older, who
have become more robust in soul through the course of their
earthly life, must have a care that the things of the Earth
should not appear all too strange to the young souls, and must
as quickly as possible help to bring to a good conclusion the
age of transition from the dying civilization to the epoch of
light that is striving to form itself anew.

Among the many tasks which Anthroposophy already has,
this will be one of the most important: to help the time of
transition to be passed quickly and overcome.

To make a start in this direction, Rudolf Steiner founded
the present Youth Section, just as the other Sections at the
Goetheanum had been founded for the seedling growth of

new endeavour in science and art fertilized by Anthroposophy. This Section of the Youth Movement must also become a starting point for the new things to which young persons look forward with such expectation, whereby the Earth will once more be able to become a true home for the young, a home where they will find again what they have experienced in pre-earthly existence.

The young are seeking, too, for the spiritual in the world of Nature, and they will be able to find it again through what Anthroposophy can bring them. And they *must* be able to find it again. The twentieth century must not be allowed to become another century of materialism. In an address to a small youth group at Koberwitz, Rudolf Steiner himself uttered these stirring words: 'If you let the twentieth century become materialistic as the nineteenth was, you will have lost much, not only of your own but of the humanity of all civilization.'

This is what the young people of today feel unconsciously when they meet together. From this unconscious knowledge, which has already become a certainty in many of them, there comes ever anew the call from the young souls: Help us to find again the spirit in Nature!

To this Anthroposophy would itself contribute inasmuch as it has something concrete to say about the spirit. It can tell about the spirit that lives everywhere in external Nature, and for present-day humanity it is also *the* key to the knowledge of this spirituality.

So we can appreciate the importance of the work of the Youth Section in the School of Spiritual Science at the Goetheanum. Out of anthroposophical understanding and experience, the Youth Section must unfold its work so as to be able to give to the Youth Movement what young people today are needing.

Hopeful and beautiful attempts have been made, and the last Youth Conference, which took place here shortly before Michaelmas, was an encouraging continuation of these beginnings. Dr Maria Röschl, leader of the Youth Section, was able once more to bring near to our young friends the living grasp of the spiritual world, with fine feeling and understanding.

The real will to live one's way into the spiritual world, which came to expression in her lectures, is the very thing that answers to the needs of the young.

In this Conference one had also the happy feeling that something can be given to the young in our Anthroposophical Society which they really value. And much was given in the many other lectures about which I cannot here speak in detail. On the side of the young there was a beautiful feeling of confident reception of all that could here be offered to them. Let us make it our concern that the Youth Movement may grow more and more into union with Anthroposophy, and go forward with it into the future. This will succeed if young people on their side also understand the words that Rudolf Steiner called out to them in Breslau in 1924: 'I would like above all to express the wish that all of you, whatever you may think and feel, may hold together with an iron will, really hold together.'

To All Members!

15 November 1925

From 25 to 28 October there was a Conference in Prague to found the Anthroposophical Society in Bohemia. Over a year ago, on the occasion of a visit by Dr Steiner to Prague after the Christmas Foundation Meeting, it was decided to found the Bohemian Society. The statutes, just as they were submitted to the authorities, have now been accepted, and so it was possible actually to found the Society on 28 October 1925.

The Bohemian Anthroposophical Society, consisting of Czech and German members, numbers about 200 to 300. Its foundation is a very significant step. We see in it the real effect of Anthroposophy. Czech and German have united in an ideal union, and have joined with gladness and enthusiasm for a common work.

From the Dornach *Vorstand*, Dr Wachsmuth and I took part in these festivities, which made a deep impression on us. It was the varied character of the members of the Bohemian *Vorstand*, appointed at the founding of their Society, which greatly interested us. With all their differences of personality there was a living unity among them.

So strong was this unity that when one of the Czech friends, Mr Brabinek, proposed as a first action of the Bohemian Society that they should undertake to bring together the complete Bohemian donation for the seating in the new Goetheanum, the proposal was adopted unanimously by the whole meeting. For us members of the Dornach *Vorstand* it was beautiful to witness this glad sense of devotion, which was no doubt awakened partly by Dr Wachsmuth's lecture on the new Goetheanum. With the pictures he showed, he made it very clear and obvious that this new Goetheanum absolutely must be completed if we as pupils of Dr Steiner are not to feel conscious of a great failure.

The last thoughts that occupied Dr Steiner had concerned the completion of the Goetheanum. It was his constant care to obtain the consent of the Swiss authorities for this tremendous building. In the very last days of his life instructions were given for the details and equipment of the building. Dr Wachsmuth spoke of this in his lecture, which preceded the meeting of the Society. Then it was that Mr Brabinek proposed they should not rest until this central building for the whole Anthroposophical Society should stand complete and ready to take on its important tasks. And as we really wish to be pupils of Dr Steiner, we will make every endeavour to erect this his monument where we shall be able to gather together from all countries to express and hear *his* teachings.

This description inflamed the hearts of Czechs and Germans alike, who had joined in this Conference of their country. All of them were ready to help and so prove themselves worthy disciples of Dr Steiner.

On 25 October the gathering was introduced with a lecture by Count Polzer-Hoditz, who through his many years' work in Prague is deeply united with the Prague groups. It was lovely that he of all people, as an old and faithful co-worker of Dr Steiner's, should open the gathering. He spoke about important impulses which had proceeded in a peculiar way, mutually complementing one another, from England and Bohemia, from Bacon and Comenius, from Wycliffe and Hus. We thus experienced the significance of Bohemia in the spiritual life of Europe.

On the evening of the same day a Class Lesson of the School of Spiritual Science could be given, and was received with real warmth and inner sympathy.

During the next days there were two lectures by Dr Wachsmuth on occult movements, and a lecture by Dr Lauer on the life-work of Dr Steiner. In between there were also many consultations on medicine, and many discussions on the work of the Society, all of which were very satisfying since they led us to hope for an excellent development of our work in the future.

Prague as the capital of Bohemia is an important centre, and significant things have taken place here. It is the threshold for crossing from East to West and from West to East; indeed, the very name 'Praha' is said to mean a threshold. If one considers how increasingly important the problem of East and West is ever becoming one can understand why Dr Steiner so often and so gladly visited Prague in spite of its distance. Through the Czechs, he sometimes said, the East must receive the light of Anthroposophy. So a great task falls to our Czech friends, for the success of which the Germans can undoubtedly render them essential help. For great tasks also require much assistance.

And for yet another reason Prague may be significant for anthroposophical endeavour. In its immediate neighbour-hood lies Karlstein Castle, the building of which was begun by Charles IV in 1348. This castle lies in a beautiful district about an hour from Prague, surrounded by four hills and steep rocky promontories.

If one studies this castle and all that is preserved for us there from the past, a history unfolds before the visitor of whose significance anthroposophists would do well to know. That such a castle could be built as a monument of the past precisely in Bohemia gives food for thought. What causes might have been working together to allow this castle, which was at the same time a cultic centre, to arise just in this district, in the very heart of Bohemia?

And then one finds, if one investigates futher, that there is a wealth of ores and siliceous crystals in Bohemia and in the mountains enclosing the country. In the west, in the Bohe-mian Forest, it is chiefly the abundance of silica crystals which is dominant in its configuration, especially in the form of pure quartz and in semi-precious stones, varied according to the metals that enter into their composition. On the other hand, to the north-west, in the Erzgebirge in the neighbourhood of Joachimstal one finds silver, gold and radioactive substances, for example the uranium ore pitchblende; to the north as far as the Silesian border, lead, tin and iron, and then, in Moravia itself, chiefly iron.

In earlier times, when the cosmic forces were able to work

even more uninterruptedly, the powers of all these minerals, and especially of the metals, exercised their influence upon Bohemia. Thus Charles IV, who was among the last of the German Emperors possessing esoteric knowledge, could feel an inner urge to build in the midst of this country, where such forces work together, a place that should serve not only as a dwelling but also for cultic purposes and for the guarding of valuable and holy relics, state documents and gems.

What strikes one immediately on a visit to the castle are its internal features. The decoration of the walls in the different chapels which are found within the castle, with their quantities of precious stones and gold, the manner in which the light is diffused through the semi-precious stones, which, set in gilded lead, take the place of window glass, lead one to conclude that Charles IV knew about the forces of precious stones and of gold.

The small Chapel of St Catherine is a real artistic gem. The entire walls as far as the dome are inlaid with semi-precious stones, such as amethyst, jasper, cornelian, agate, and so on, while the cross-vaulting above has a blue background, adorned with gold rosettes according to Rosicrucian motifs. Here, according to tradition, Charles IV would every year withdraw from Good Friday to Easter Sunday so as to be able to give himself over to his meditations in undisturbed seclusion.

However, to describe everything else of abundant beauty that is still to be seen in Karlstein Castle would here be too much; so mention will only be made of what is important to us. We come therefore to a tower connected by a bridge to the castle, which, separated from the actual palace, lies like a strong fortress on a height somewhat further away, and towers over the whole. Right at the top of the tower may be found the Chapel of the Holy Cross. The stairway leading up the tower to this chapel is adorned with frescoes on the walls, supposed to represent the life of St Ludmila on the right side and on the left the life of St Wenceslas, the ruler of Bohemia, who was martyred in the year 936 and since that time has been looked upon as the patron saint of Prague.

Dr Steiner once said of these frescoes that they represented the Chymical Wedding of Christian Rosenkreuz in a primitive form, and in looking at the pictures one can well recognize the various phases of the Chymical Wedding, for example the picture of the setting-free of the prisoner in chains, and his release from the tower, or the representation of St Wenceslas sowing seed in the night, harvesting, and himself threshing the corn, then milling the wheat and baking from this the sacred wafers. All this represents an alchemical process, carried out during the night, a process connected with Earth, Air, Fire and Water. Then comes the picture of the burial of the dead. One also recognizes, in the picture where St Wenceslas is serving out the food to the invited guests, the invitation to the marriage feast, and one can also see how the picture of the last supper in the life of St Wenceslas is taken from the feast of the worthy and unworthy spiritual seekers in the Chymical Wedding. And finally there is the execution of St Wenceslas, in which the beheading, the piercing with the spear, and the dismembering of his body are reminiscent of initiation experiences.

After the ascent of the tower one arrives, as already stated, at a chapel—a Grail chapel—which is called in Karlstein the Chapel of the Holy Cross. And likewise we know from words of Dr Steiner's that here we really have before us a kind of chapel of the Grail.

This ascent from the way of initiation to the Grail above is magnificent. This chapel shines before us in wonderful splendour. The windows are formed of mounted stones—pure topazes, amethysts and almandines—the entire roof is gilded, and represents the vault of Heaven, with Sun, Moon and many stars, interspersed with the previously described rosettes. The walls are inlaid from the floor upwards, to a height of over a metre, with polished semi-precious stones, with amethysts, cornelians, agates and jaspers, and above that as further wall decoration may still be found many pictures. All this makes an overwhelming impression.

So from what has been described it can be looked upon as certain that the personality of St Wenceslas was connected in some way with Christian Rosenkreuz, and if one compares still further the life of St Wenceslas with true Rosicrucianism,

the same analogies may everywhere be found. In St Wenceslas, the patron saint of Prague, who died on St Michael's
Day, 29 September 936, there shines before us the figure of a
true Rosicrucian. Michael too stood near his being; and when
we realize that St George's Church in Prague dates also from
this period, then indeed Prague is rightly today of great
interest for us as the centre of a spiritual stream.

The Being of Man and the Season of Michaelmas

September 1926

In an important lecture about Michael, given at Dornach in October 1923, Rudolf Steiner spoke about the significant way in which the Archangel Michael works in human life and in the evolution of culture and of the world. He summarized this whole work of Michael in the following verse, in words which are brought down from spiritual heights and may be found inscribed in the astral light of the cosmos:

O Man,
Thou mouldest it to thy service,
Thou revealest it according to the value of its substance
In many of thy works.
Yet it will only bring thee healing,
When to thee is revealed
Its lofty spirit-potency.

And now at Michaelmas one must try to understand and really experience what is going on at this season, the autumn season of Michaelmas, in the universe—the macrocosm—and in the human being—the microcosm. To concern ourselves at present with these things is the task of any individual who has the will to stand in the true sense in the spiritual culture of our age, in which Michael has the leadership and is striving to bestow his Impulses on mankind.

A proper understanding of Michael will also be of enormous value for those who are concerned with the riddles of the art of healing, and who are in earnest about the knowledge of healing influences in the human being. So we will have to ask ourselves what this actually is that is said to reveal itself in substance for the service of mankind but yet can only be for the healing of man when he can know it in its spiritual nature.

Now if we make clear to ourselves what the development of present-day culture shows, it is matter, substance, that governs human interest. We live in a culture that only recognizes as reality the visible and material, in which men apply all their energy and thought to the control and manipulation of earthly substances. The spiritual in matter has no longer that significance for present-day consciousness which it had in earlier times, in previous cultures. And we are living in an age of machines, where people detached from everything spiritual work on matter and wish to subject it to their earthly needs. It is precisely machines and what is connected with them which is present before us as an essential cultural factor, and so we are directed to iron as to one of the most important substances of our time. Iron stands in our service and reveals itself in our inventions as substance.

This lending oneself to matter, uniting oneself to matter and using it for one's own purposes, has been necessary for mankind's evolution. But we are now living at a point in time when the human being, while acknowledging the achievements of this way of thinking, must come to grasp and experience the spirit which is at work behind matter. Should he not succeed in uniting himself again with this spirituality, then he would fall under the spell of the world which he has himself despiritualized, through which the Ahrimanic beings could gain ever greater and greater influence.

This danger will be avoided by man if he can again open up in himself a sense for Michael's mission in human evolution. Then he will learn to understand how the spiritualization of our culture is connected with the working of Michael. He will learn to experience how this iron from which present-day culture forges its machines is related to that substance which falls down to the Earth as meteoric iron from the world of the stars. This substance condensed to meteoric iron is spiritually connected with the force which in the cosmos forms itself into the sword used by Michael in his battle against materialism, through which the Dragon is striving to take possession of the Earth and of man.

What takes place in the environment of the Earth as a huge battle between heavenly and earthly powers is also reflected in man, the microcosmic image of the macrocosm.

In what way is the microcosm affected by this battle?

Here one must learn to understand how the human being is placed between Heaven and Earth, how earthly and cosmic forces work into him and come to operation inside him. Then one sees how these influences may be recognized in the physiological processes of one's organism and in the manifestations of one's thinking, feeling and willing. We must experience as threefold the physiological life-processes that are at work in our organism in the lower man, the head-man, and the middle man. So one may speak of a sulphur-process, which is a kind of combustion process, in which the metabolic functions and everything connected with them take place. It may be compared with the process of blossoming in the plant, and arises from the interplay between physical-ethereal processes and astral influences.

Now the blossoming of a plant may also be described as a kind of animal-forming process that has been arrested in its genesis. But because the astral world only works upon the plant from outside, this process does not come to the point of functioning in the plant as it does in the animal organism with its digestion, breathing and blood-formation. And whereas in the plant one can only speak of a tendency towards animalization, in the human being one has the process of animal-formation itself in all these functions, actively shared in by the astral body inside him. That this animal-forming process in the lower man is held back within the prescribed limits is thanks to the ego, which raises us as human beings above the animal level. In his metabolic-limb system man is in addition intimately connected with the earthly forces.

The upper man, the nerves-and-senses system, is on the other hand related to the forces from beyond the Earth, to the forces of the stars. But at the same time there also take place in the nerves-and-senses system processes of destruction that may be compared with the mineralizing, salt-forming processes in outer nature, and which the human organism needs in order that man may attain conscious experience.

In between, in the middle or rhythmic man, work the so-called mercurial processes that operate in the breathing and circulation of the blood and are related to the forces found in the surroundings of the Earth, the forces of light and air. The mercurial element in the human being may also be regarded as the factor that holds the balance in his organism between lightness and gravity, between influences from the earth and those from beyond the earth.

These three processes are continually at work in the human organism, and the health of man is the expression of their harmonious interplay within him. And if one or other of these life-processes is able to gain the upper hand, illness is the result.

Now in the course of the year these physiological functions in the human being are also influenced in various ways by the different seasons. Thus in wintertime the salt-processes come more into the foreground, and this is connected with a more conscious life, one expressing itself less in outward activity. Man leads a life that is more turned inwards, and has the possibility of approaching the riddles of existence with more subtle thinking.

In summertime an enhancement of the sulphur-process sets in, reaching its culmination at midsummer. Man also feels inwardly an intensification of his life-processes; his devotion to outer life is stimulated and the earthly forces in his being assert themselves more strongly. On the other hand, this is connected with a damping down of consciousness; when the metabolic processes preponderate, man is less clear in his thinking, and is in danger of losing himself in a dream-like condition. In summertime, when his astral body becomes outwardly more and more radiant on account of the intensified combustion processes, dragon and serpent forms rise up from the earth in an attempt to come to life in these sulphur-processes, to cloud human consciousness completely and take possession of it.

In this danger the Gods come to the side of men, bestowing helping forces in order to strengthen human consciousness.

Michael with his helping hosts is there, coming to man's aid during the autumn season. The sulphur-processes arising from the earth are counteracted by the power of meteoric iron, which during this season may be observed in the heavens in multitudes of shooting stars. With the spiritual power of iron, Michael fights against the uprising Dragon. And it is the iron sword of Michael which, as a cosmic healing power, does battle with the Ahrimanic beings who are striving to creep into the enhanced sulphuric-processes, and liberates man from the anxiety and fear which always arise in him when his consciousness can no longer work clearly.

What is really happening inside the human organism when this battle of Michael with the Dragon is being waged in the astral world? A process of marvellous complexity is actually at work at this time. The blood streaming through the whole body and containing the red corpuscles is saturated with the forces of iron. The organism is enabled to absorb more iron and unite it with the haemoglobin. And what happens in the cosmos when the meteors shoot through the heavens like radiant darts from the stars, preventing the Ahrimanic beings from arising and spreading abroad, takes place in miniature through the strengthened iron-process in the blood. Since in the time of autumn man's forces of soul and spirit are newly awakened in him, he is also able to increase accordingly the strength of the iron-forces in his blood and to set them up against the sulphur-processes that are striving to flood his being. The organism is saturated as if with numberless tiny meteors through the iron-laden red corpuscles in the blood. Thus the whole organism is permeated with a healing force and freed from all disease-bringing factors and from the elements of anxiety and fear.

This anxiety and fear is often only experienced unconsciously, but it may also express itself in moods of depression or itself lead to physical fatigue and exhaustion if the organism is not in a position to call up sufficient iron-forces for its protection. A doctor who knows these processes in the human being will be able to come to the assistance of nature in such cases by the administration of iron.

What thus happens within the human organism in the great

rhythm of the year, like a flow and ebb of health and disease-
bringing influences induced by living together with the processes of surrounding Nature, is also visibly reflected in man's
daily rhythm of sleeping and waking life. In sleep, where
conscious activity comes to rest, where ego and astral body are
drawn out, the metabolic system sets up an active upbuilding
process in the ether body and physical body, whereas in
conscious waking life the destructive forces are more strongly
at work. A danger is also continually hidden in this daily
repeated interplay of the upper and lower processes in the
human organism, if a man is not in a position to create a
healthy balance by means of those processes that are connected with his activity in the ego and astral body.

In order that this danger may be daily overcome, man has
the iron circulating in his blood. Without this iron the blood
would always be diseased, and by means of iron a wonderful
healing process continually takes place in the blood in a quite
natural way. Through the radiant force of the iron, the
metabolic process must constantly be held within its healthy
limits, and what works upwards in the blood as sulphur-
processes must be balanced out, otherwise the human being
would become ill. And apart from anaemia, there are still
other manifestations of disease that are fundamentally connected with the fact that the organism lacks sufficient iron-
forces to protect itself against the influences originating in the
metabolism.

So what is working every day physiologically in the human
organism undergoes an enhancement in the course of the
summer until the time of autumn. And in olden times, when
man still had the capacity to feel his way into what was going
on both in him and around him, he experienced the time of
Michaelmas with its helpful forces as a festival season when he
could celebrate his release by Michael from the danger
through which Ahriman was threatening to engulf him. Present-day man should also re-acquire this. He should learn to
experience in a new way how Michael is trying to help him
towards inner freedom and can liberate him from anxiety and
fear, and also how the powers of Michael are powers of
healing. Out of his own will man should consciously reunite

with what is working in the universe and in himself as the power of Michael. Then as Regent of the Age, Michael will also be able to unite himself with us human beings and bestow his Impulses on mankind. And the time will come when we can celebrate the Michael festival in a way truly appropriate to our Age.

Report on the Conferences in Jena and in Holland

21 November 1926

Dr Vreede and I were able to attend two meetings, the Conference of the Anthroposophical Society of Central Germany in Jena and the International Anthroposophical Education Congress in Holland, and we have pleasure in reporting that both these conferences went off extremely well and harmoniously.

During this autumn Conference, from 22 to 24 October, members from the whole of Thuringia were assembled in Jena, in the heart of Germany. It was chiefly a meeting of a smaller circle, and yet, considering the number of members in the country, the attendance was good and it was a pleasure to be present. There was a warm and hearty atmosphere.

We also felt strongly the importance of the fact that such a meeting as this took place in Jena—a sign that new spiritual life is once again unfolding here. We must still feel that even today Jena is a centre of spiritual life—Jena, the town of Ernst Haeckel, with which so many important great figures in the intellectual development of mankind are connected: Goethe, Schiller, Fichte, Hegel, Novalis, Wilhelm von Humboldt. It is also a town that chose the Archangel Michael as its patron saint. And does the spiritual history of Jena not show, as Rudolf Steiner pointed out to us, how it was predestined to pour into our evolution what was needed for the individual development of man as is demanded by our time?

With particularly great joy we greeted the fact that so strong a nucleus of anthroposophical life had come into existence at this spot. Notwithstanding the great variety of presentations, the general atmosphere of the Conference was uniform in spirit, this unity being born out of the enthusiasm for all that the Conference was offering to its members. This unity of spirit permeated all its members and linked them to one another. All that was presented to them was received with an open and a grateful heart.

Dr Vreede gave two lectures. In the first she spoke about the relation of astronomy to Anthroposophy. In the second she dealt with the natural and moral order of the cosmos, opening out a vista of their future reunion (a result of scientific research on anthroposophical lines). She succeeded in showing us in an exceedingly interesting way the intimate interaction of cosmic and terrestrial happenings.

Dr Stein gave two lectures of absorbing interest on the history of the Grail, in which he pursued the traces of that spiritual current with which it is connected. His exposition was supported and illustrated by a vast body of evidence, which in itself will provide a great impulse to further investigation. And the peculiarly delightful feature of Dr Stein's lectures was that they were so full of stimulus and incentive, kindling enthusiasm for the study of history.

After him, Siegfried Pickert, one of the representatives of curative education as practised at the Lauenstein centre, gave a talk. In a truly moving way he drew a picture of the diagnosis and treatment of children who are backward in their development. His lecture radiated forth a love for humanity, permeated by spiritual knowledge, which leads man to helpful deeds. Herr Pickert gave us an account of the curative educational work carried on at Lauenstein, a work which has met with such appreciation that it has been necessary to enlarge the establishment after two years of its existence. Lieut-Colonel Seebohm has been kind enough to place Haus Bernhard (Jena-Zwätzen) at its disposal.

Dr Unger spoke with warm words about the present position of the Goetheanum, and made a deep impression on all who were present as to the significance of the Goetheanum building and our own responsibility towards it. In the course of the Conference—generally in the early morning—three lessons of the First Class were given by me. It should be emphasized that the deeply satisfactory achievement of the

Conference is mainly due to the efforts of Lieut-Colonel Seebohm. As leader of the Jena group he was chairman of the meeting, and his concluding words gave the Conference a dignified ending. He had succeeded in winning the hearts of young and old.

★   ★   ★

The second gathering, the International Congress for Anthroposophical Education, took place from 28 October to 5 November at the Hague. Whereas the meeting in Thuringia bore something of a local stamp, this Congress in Holland displayed an entirely international character.

In addition to the Dutch members and those in Holland who are interested in the work, friends from Germany, England and Switzerland who are interested in the educational system of Rudolf Steiner were also present. For this Congress it had been possible to obtain, right in the centre of the Hague, accomodation very specially suited to the exhibition of the children's work. This accomodation, all under the same roof, comprised a large lecture-hall and a smaller hall with refreshment room, so the Congress offered every comfort to the visitors and made an impression of quite remarkable unity.

To start off, Dr Zeylmans held a solemn opening of the Congress in a smaller circle of active participants including the members of the *Vorstand* who were present. A living picture of Rudolf Steiner was placed before us by Dr Zeylmans, who spoke of his continued presence and activity among us. There followed the public and official opening of the Congress at which several distinguished Dutch educational authorities were present. Then Dr Zeylmans gave a lecture entitled 'The Educational Demands of our Age'. This lecture and the general opening address were held in the Dutch language. After this came a visit to the exhibition of children's work, which was repeated regularly every day.

The exhibition, which filled three large and two smaller rooms, contained work from children of the Waldorf School in Stuttgart, the Continuation School at the Goetheanum, the German schools in Essen and Hamburg, the New School in

London, the Priory School in King's Langley and the Vrije School at the Hague. Here were to be seen examples from the work of the painting classes, modelling classes, and from the classes in the various branches of handicrafts. Work was also shown from the institutes devoted to curative education, Lauenstein in Jena and from the children's home Sonnenhof in Arlesheim.

Special interest was manifested in this exhibition. It attracted many visitors, to whom everything was explained by the teachers present in the different rooms for that purpose. It was very interesting to listen to the many questions dealing with the educational methods of Rudolf Steiner, and to see from the whole manner in which these questions were put how much understanding for these educational problems already exists in the external world. The number of visitors reached its highest point during the last two days.

For those people also who have entered more deeply into these educational methods this exhibition was most instructive. One could see how far advanced the children of the Waldorf School, which has existed already seven years, are in their work, compared to the children of the younger schools. Also one could observe the markedly individual character of the different schools. One could see, for instance, how the paintings of the children from the Dutch school entered more into the plant-like, watery element, thus corresponding to the dominant character of the surrounding nature. The paintings from the Essen school, on the other hand, showed very clearly how the children living in this town, with its decidedly industrial character, have great difficulty in experiencing colours. It could also be clearly seen that, though many children come to this school with pathological tendencies, through the method of teaching they are gradually cured of their unhealthy symptoms. In the work of the children this healing process could be traced stage by stage.

Of specially deep interest were the explanations Herr Wolffhügel was able to give in this connection. And of especial interest once again were the explanations by Herr Pickert who, as in the Jena Conference, gave a lecture based on practical experience in curative education. With paintings by sick children in Lauenstein and Sonnenhof, he showed how clearly the healing process can be observed and traced in such cases.

The work of the Continuation School at the Goetheanum revealed a more mature art, enabling one to divine what high faculties the Waldorf method may yet succeed in unfolding. This work was mostly by older children and one could feel how much they were assisted by living in the midst of keen artistic activity.

Most interesting was a special department for children's toys, designed and made in the school workshop by Herr Wolffhügel and lately reproduced and put on the market by the Waldorf-Spielzeug and Verlag GmbH in Stuttgart.

A special joy in the course of this Conference was a eurythmy demonstration by children of the Vrije School and the Waldorf School in the Schouwberg. Tickets were sold out and the children had a hearty reception. Great interest was shown in a gymnastic display by Count Bothmer with pupils from the Waldorf School, an art for which the first indications were given by Dr Steiner and which has been excellently elaborated by Count Bothmer. It was a favourable sign that he was invited to repeat the display in the Academy of Physical Culture in Amsterdam.

Needless to say, the Conference was a great joy for these children. Beside Amsterdam they were able to visit Delft and Leyden. It was a great experience for them to make acquaintance with such altogether different conditions by their journey. After the gymnastic display they and their teachers received a very warm address, thanking them for their visit. Little presents were given to them and in happily chosen words they were told of the value of such journeys in learning to know and love other countries and regions of the Earth. Dr Zeylmans spoke to them of how Holland rose out of the sea, how it was literally wrested bit by bit from the sea by its inhabitants.

Much could still be said on what was given in the various lectures, but we cannot go into further detail. Every one of them awakened real interest. Dr von Heydebrand was able once more to call forth a true and living image of our dear teacher, speaking on 'Rudolf Steiner as an Educator'. Immensely interesting was the lecture by Herr Wolffhügel on the handicraft lessons in the Waldorf School. Next evening Dr Stein spoke about the history lessons, showing how they can become a source of living strength for the fulfilment of the tasks of mankind in our age, a subject whereby he was able to carry his whole audience with him in living enthusiasm.

Although Herr Rutz's lecture, 'The Methods of Teaching Art in the Lower Classes of the Waldorf School', lasted some two hours, the fact that everyone would gladly have listened much longer proves how interesting it was. It was followed by a lecture by Dr Kolisko on the art of healing in relation to education, in which he tried, among other things, to show what great interest Dr Steiner's education should be to the doctor whose duty it is to help children.

As was to be expected, Dr von Baravalle's lecture, 'The Teaching of Geometry and the Training of Thought', was as usual sparkling with life. And once more Dr von Baravalle succeeded by his new interpretation of mathematics in arousing the enthusiasm of each member of his audience, even those who had hitherto understood but little of mathematics. As the last in the series of evening lectures, Dr Schwebsch spoke on 'Aesthetic Education'. He dealt with the different arts, giving a wide survey of the teaching of aesthetics, and showing what can be gained for aesthetic education by a spiritual-scientific study of the arts.

The afternoon lectures by Dr Lehrs, Herr Paul Baumann, Herr Max Stibbe, Mr C. Harwood, Herr van t'Hoff and Dr Blass, concluding with the above-mentioned lecture on 'Anthroposophical Curative Education' by Herr Pickert, offered extremely interesting contributions and were very well received.

With all this, real anthroposophical life was not neglected, and opportunity was given for attending Class Lessons, which were held during the mornings.

The whole Congress ended with a brilliant and well attended soirée; everyone was in happy mood. At intervals during the evening we were entertained by pianoforte solos by Walter Rummel, whom we are always so glad to hear, and by excellent recitations of some of Goethe's poems by Fräulein Zaiser. A surprise, announced in a humorous address by Dr Zeylmans, proved to be a pamphlet on the Vrije School at the Hague, which will serve at the same time as a prospectus of the school.

We may therefore say with much pleasure and gratitude that both the Conference in Jena and the Congress in the Hague passed off satisfactorily and happily, and that good results are to be expected from them for the future.

The International Summer School in Scotland (Gareloch, Dumbartonshire)

26 June 1927

I am writing these lines in order, on the one hand, to awaken an understanding with regard to the Summer School that is shortly to be held in Scotland, and, on the other hand, to prevent misunderstandings that may threaten to arise here and there because not everyone realizes what is really intended.

The previous Summer Schools at Penmaenmawr and Torquay sprang, like this coming one, out of Mr Dunlop's initiative, and, as everyone who took part in them knows, they were crowned with great success. The most wonderful lectures were delivered there by Rudolf Steiner, lectures that were also available for non-Anthroposophists and dealt with initiation science. Things could be expressed differently there than in other places. It was as though the understanding for the spiritual world were more open, as though it were more possible for the listeners, even though they had come from other places, to respond to the more delicate impulses that they could everywhere hear coming towards them out of Nature, and to mount in their feelings to the realms of soul and spirit. And anybody who at that time had the good fortune to have one or more conversations with Rudolf Steiner will know how something special also rang there in harmony with his words, something that lay in the atmosphere and gave a special tone to the conversations. Primeval wisdom, primeval tradition hovered in the environment. It was as though—and many friends who were there could experience it—this ancient wisdom were awakened out of deep sleep by the spoken words of Rudolf Steiner. Anthroposophy thereby gained an even deeper radiance than it already had. The living and weaving of the spirit within the physical, of which Anthroposophy teaches, was more deeply perceived. One felt oneself drawn nearer to the spiritual, although even to these places present-day civilization had found entry and one was living in the midst of its conditions.

And here I would also like to mention something that Rudolf Steiner felt to be so very important for us as Anthroposophists, and which came to expression in conversation in this way: that Michael, the Spirit of the Age, under whose leadership we stand, will more and more demand that we take Anthroposophy out into the whole world, and that cosmopolitanism should take the place of remaining narrowly bounded within a mystery centre. And for single individuals too it is exceedingly important to go out and learn something of the outer world because, so Rudolf Steiner said, a true knowledge of the outer world makes it possible for human beings also to come to understand the spiritual world in the proper way during the time between death and a new birth. And upon this proper knowledge of the spiritual world will also depend our ability to know our own organism. If we have this knowledge of our own organism, then, when we next come down to the physical world and choose a physical body for our incarnation, we shall be able to choose one that is free from inherited defects, or we shall be so strong in soul and spirit that we shall have the forces in us to overcome the so-called inherited body and to build up those organs with which the soul and spirit can live in harmony. It was for this reason that, in the old mysteries, those who were to be initiated were recommended to undertake great journeys and travels, so as to come to know the manifoldness of the world, to feel the contrast between the regions of coldness and moisture, on the one hand, and those of dryness and heat, on the other, and to take into themselves all intermediate conditions. Many people at the present time have to struggle with the fact that their soul and spirit cannot always make full use of their physical body. This is because between today and the time of those journeys, when the mysteries also had their period of blossoming, the Christian Middle Ages intervened with their cloistered life, which bound men more to their native soil. And only where something of this ancient knowledge still survived was this 'sticking to one's roots' broken through.

It is of great importance for the coming century that men should once more win through to the possibility of building up such physical bodies as their whole spiritual being can properly connect itself with. Naturally a real knowledge of the outer world is not only to be gained through journeys and travels but also through an intimate, loving penetration into the secrets of Nature; nevertheless, it is important to become acquainted with foreign lands and customs.

And now let us once more come back to the Summer Schools. It was certainly to Mr Dunlop's credit that in a sensitive manner he selected places for the Summer Schools in whose immediate neighbourhood the primeval wisdom had held sway thousands of years ago. In Penmaenmawr, lying on the west coast of England, opposite Ireland, the Druidic Mysteries had flowered; in Cornwall, not far from Torquay, the ruins of King Arthur's castle were to be found, from where King Arthur and his knights carried their activities into the world. And this year the choice falls on Scotland, so rich in legendary lore, at a place from which those islands known as the Hebrides can easily be reached, such as Iona, and Staffa, where lies the famous Fingal's Cave. Now in a lecture given in 1909 in Berlin, after he had previously heard in a concert Mendelsohn's Overture *The Hebrides*, Rudolf Steiner reminded his listeners of the mysterious destinies of prehistoric people that were played out upon these islands. These prehistoric people, who had wandered over there from Atlantis, had preserved in their Celtic descendants the old Atlantean clairvoyance in its absolutely pristine condition. And he spoke of how these Celtic peoples, who were found there in Ireland, in Scotland and on the intermediate groups of islands, felt themselves still wholly bound up with the world of the Gods, and by these they let themselves be guided and advised. Whoever still had the full power of his seership was the leader of his people. Such was Fingal, of many legends, whose famous deeds were sung by his son, the blind bard Ossian, who seems to us like a Homer of the West. 'And we can understand,' says Rudolf Steiner in this lecture, 'that the revival of these Ossianic chants, through Macpherson in the eighteenth century, made a tremendous impression on Europe. Goethe, Herder and Napoleon believed that they could hear in their tones something of the magic of primeval days.'

Yes indeed, one can feel in these chants the magic of primeval wisdom, the wisdom that speaks in wind and cloud, in mist and lightning, in Moon and stars. All this is cosmic wisdom, which was sung there in chants at nightly gatherings by the bards, who as initiates still had in their souls the last remnants of Druidic Mysteries. And Fingal's dwelling place, now known as Fingal's Cave, was felt to be a cathedral crystallized out of Nature itself, where pillar after pillar towers up in rows of tremendous stone formations, above them an arching roof of the same stonework, and all washed by the waters of the sea, beating against the columns in waves.

One can indeed feel thrilled at the thought of being able to go to such a place as this, bearing Anthroposophy in one's heart. And if the right words can be found in which to express what we there have to say, then Rudolf Steiner's spirit will be beside us, and help us to carry true Anthroposophy to a place where as yet it is but little known.

Therefore it was a great joy to the Medical Section to be invited to take part in this Summer School—not only because it is delightful to visit and get to know other countries, but also because one of the most important impulses given by Rudolf Steiner can thereby be realized.

The Summer School in Scotland

4 September 1927

From 25 July to 5 August, a Summer School took place at Gareloch (Dumbartonshire), on the subject of 'Health and Disease'. The School was held in an hotel, surrounded by a beautiful park, on the shores of one of those seawater lakes that were once fjords.

It was thus possible for the whole Conference and the meetings among its members to be concentrated in one building. And so for 10 days, the 150 to 160 people who came to the Conference, filled with a great longing for a spiritual impulse, were able to be constantly together and live a life directed to a common goal. In spite of all the differences of nationality, the days passed in such harmony that all could feel the higher spiritual reality underlying this 'community life'.

The aim of the Summer School was to study anthroposophical medicine, so a large share of the work devolved upon the Medical Section of the Goetheanum whose task it is to spread over the world a knowledge of the teachings given by Rudolf Steiner for an extension of the art of healing. This makes it essential that the representatives of this medical work shall themselves get to know the world, and they joyfully took advantage of the opportunity thus offered them, to visit and make a study of a foreign country. A medical movement taking its start from spiritual science must, among other things, be able to lay the basis of a *geographical science of medicine*, which is built up on the principles of anthroposophical knowledge of universe, Earth and man. It is known to science that diseases may appear in different forms in the various zones of the Earth, and also that in the various regions of the Earth certain illnesses may be found more rarely, others again more commonly. Human beings, too, react differently in the particular regions and their possibilities of being healed vary considerably.

Now spiritual science teaches us to understand what these phenomena are based on—teaches us, for instance, in what way the conditions of the soil, the water and the air, and warmth, affect the human being and how they specially influence particular organs.

So it is important for a doctor to be able to study these conditions in the places themselves, and from this point of view to travel and learn about foreign countries.

This geographical medicine, which at the same time is also a medicine of the mysteries, must gradually be more and more developed, since numerous valuable indications in this regard have been given to us by Rudolf Steiner. This thought also underlay the participation of the Medical Section in the organization of the Summer School in Scotland, and we are indeed enormously grateful that the friends in England have given us such opportunities.

From start to finish the event took place in a unified manner and was pervaded by a mood of seriousness but also of happiness; every day there was eager expectancy as to what would be given.

Over and above the lectures announced on the programme, the leaders of the Conference desired to introduce something centrally anthroposophical, with the object of deepening what was said about medicine and education, and of preparing the right mood for the planned visit to the Mystery Centres of Iona and Staffa at the conclusion of the Conference. To this end, choice fell on the subject of the history of the mysteries in the different ages, and lectures were prepared together by a group of people there who had already given much study to this subject and had had access to the indications given by Rudolf Steiner in this connection. Two lectures were given in the mornings and usually one in the evenings. The afternoons were free—in so far as they were not taken up with medical discussions about practical questions, or other meetings—so that one could allow the influence of the surroundings, with all their beauty and natural characteristics, to come to full effect.

The vegetation was most strange, almost tropically luxuriant, but yet much greener and richer in sap than in the south, and for this reason exceptionally beneficial to the health. One had the feeling of being enwoven in a rich and still unspent ethereal world, and could understand why the people in this region are of a more dreamy nature, and indeed sometimes give the impression of simple-mindedness, while at the same time many of them still have the faculty of atavistic clairvoyance known as 'second sight'. The tendency of the population to drink a lot of alcohol is also partly related to the desire to expel this second sight for fear of such experiences.

So far as the lectures themselves were concerned, let it quite briefly be said that everyone gave of their best. Most of the lectures were given in English and the others were splendidly translated from German by Mr George Kaufmann. It would lead too far to give a detailed account of each lecture and a few points only can be mentioned. Fundamental principles in connection with the metals, their relation to physiological processes, and metal-therapy were dealt with by Dr Eugen Kolisko and myself. Frau Doctor Kolisko spoke of her experiments in connection with the influences of the planets on the metals. This aroused the very greatest interest and made a really wonderful impression on the practical minds of the English—Frau Doctor Kolisko was besieged with requests for private interviews where further questions might be asked and more information given. And it was helpful to be together in the hotel after the lectures, for groups gathered everywhere to talk about what had been said and to learn more. In this way the different nationalities came into intimate contact with one another.

Dr Zeylmans's lecture, 'Psychoanalysis from the Point of View of Spiritual Science', was very opportune, for everyone today is thinking about this question. The treatment of the problem was more especially valuable and useful for doctors who had not yet come into our movement. From other points of view, Dr Glas continued this subject in his lectures on 'Sleep and Dreams'. That Rudolf Steiner's art of education is filled with a healing quality was shown in the lectures given by Dr Baravalle, Dr Kolisko and Dr Karl Schubert—the latter dealing more especially with the education of abnormal children.

Again Dr Vreede gave a most interesting lecture about the Moon and its relation to man, and this was a splendid continuation of what had already been said about the working of planets and metals.

Dr Staunton spoke on the history of medicine and Mrs Dank about food in different countries, dealing, as well, with certain problems of folk psychology. The social question is intimately connected with medicine and education, and Mr George Kaufmann gave two lectures on the way in which modern social conditions are prone to injure the health of mankind. He then led on to the healing of these social conditions by Rudolf Steiner's teaching of the Threefold Commonwealth.

The series of lectures was concluded by one from Mr Dunlop. He gave a picture of human life and spoke of the life-work of Dr Steiner in words of warm gratitude, showing how this offers the solution of so many problems. He directed the thoughts of his audience to the Dornach hill and to the new Goetheanum, and his words revealed a deep sense of responsibility that all our strivings must be in the direction of building a path along which those who stand outside our movement may find their way to the Goetheanum. In this connection he spoke of the plan he had personally discussed with Dr Steiner, of creating an opportunity for placing before the world the solutions offered by Anthroposophy of great world problems—to the end that from all countries people may be led to the Goetheanum as the centre of our movement. He spoke about the World Conference which it is proposed to hold in London next July and August. This address made a deep impression on all the members of the Conference. At the conclusion of the Conference Mrs Merry gave a beautiful lecture, with lantern slides, on Iona and the life of St Columba, and his significance in Christianity.

It was very encouraging to find among the members of the Conference doctors from very many different countries—

from the south, east and west of Germany, Austria, north and south of Switzerland, Portugal, Sweden, England and Scotland. I mention this in order to show that anthroposophical medicine has already taken root in many lands. The results of practical experience and the indications given to all these doctors and students in personal interviews will surely have fallen on fertile soil. Our treatment for carcinoma, for instance, was the subject of certain special conversations, as also was curative eurythmy in connection with a lecture by Dr Bockholt.

After the Conference had passed in such a delightful and happy way, we set out on the excursion to the two islands of Iona and Staffa, which belong to the Hebrides.

Iona, the dwelling-place of the Irish monk Columba, is known as the first Christian settlement in the North. It was previously an old Druid sanctuary. From Iona, Christianity began to spread over Scotland to the Continent, and the younger Columba and St Gallus, pupils of St Columba, came as far as present-day St Gallen in Switzerland. The elder Columba, who may be regarded as the 'teacher of teachers', was connected with Druidic Mysteries in Ireland, where his birthplace lies. These he had to give up when, following a new impulse, he was prompted to leave Ireland and, seeking for a new home, he came to the island of Iona, whose former name was Hu. Since we know from Rudolf Steiner that Hu was connected with Flos, the name of the inspirer of esoteric Christianity, this is an indication that Columba also stood under the leadership of Flos. Seen in this light, Iona became for us a place full of significance. The island itself is both lovely and health-bringing, and the traces of its mighty past are still very alive.

Staffa makes quite a different impression. This island arose in the last period of the Tertiary epoch, that is to say, in late Atlantean times, and it forms an important part of that great 'basalt bridge' which starts from Ireland, stretches under the sea and here and there rises above the waters. The sight of the black, six-sided basalt pillars rising out of the sea makes a most wonderful impression; they stand there like a memorial of mighty titanic forces working upwards from the depth of the Earth. There are four cave formations on this island, and we were able to visit the largest of these. Passing through a corridor of one basalt pillar after another along the cliff wall, one comes to a cave, Fingal's Cave. Around an angle of rock rises this wonderful 'cathedral' of Nature, with the surging sea for its floor, the dark basalt pillars for its walls and sandstone—flowing in Gothic curves—for its roof. This cave was once used as a place of initiation by Fingal and his heroes, of whose deeds Fingal's son, the Bard Ossian, has sung so beautifully. It is said that the heroes who were to be initiated into the 'Mysteries of the Depths' were given over to the tides of the sea in a little boat, without rudder or helm. For three-and-a-half days the boat was left in the cave and whoever lay in it experienced the thundering and surging of the waters, which poured with such might into the cave that the whole mountain resounded.

Whoever passed through this initiation had to undergo experiences of endless terror, and if in three-and-a-half days his courage was not broken, and the waves again carried his boat out of the cave, so that he could wake to a new life, then he had passed the test. Whoever did not pass this test either perished in the cave or emerged shattered in body and soul.

As one stood in the cave with this in mind, and listened to the terrifying roar of the surging waters, one could imagine the experiences of those souls who were given over here in dreadful loneliness to the struggle with the elements.

These things also give us a picture of customs originating in an age long before Columba's arrival in Iona. They give us a glimpse of the terrible trials through which one had to pass if one strove to become a Druid initiate. Columba too, as previously mentioned, was already connected from Ireland with this Druid culture, traces of which still survive to this day. And so it was really overwhelming to experience so closely together the two contrasting effects presented to us by Iona and Staffa. With heightened feeling we left the islands, and when we all met together again our souls were the richer by a great experience.

The World Conference on the Spiritual Science of Rudolf Steiner (London, 20 July to 1 August 1928)

19 August 1928

Four years ago a conversation took place between Dr Steiner and Mr Dunlop that was the starting point for the undertaking of this Conference. It was during this conversation that the question arose as to how such organizations as the Summer Schools at Penmaenmawr and Torquay, which had been arranged by Mr Dunlop with Mrs Merry's help, could be continued on a larger scale.

Thus arose the idea for the World Conference. It was conceived as an opportunity for putting forward, in one of the great capitals of the West, the fundamental impulse of the Goetheanum: to bring all nations together on a universal spiritual footing. For it is indeed the task of those who desire to uphold the spiritual life of mankind to prepare a common ground for it, not only in Middle Europe but also in the East and in the West.

Rudolf Steiner very much wished to consolidate this impulse. And much as he felt, and expressed, his satisfaction over the Summer Schools, he declared nevertheless that the intention of the Summer Schools must be continued on a wider foundation until it gradually became world-wide. For everything connected with the Goetheanum was regarded in a world sense. So Mr Dunlop was tirelessly active in promoting it.

In spite of all the difficulties that arose because many were of the opinion that it was still too soon to give the idea a world-wide form, it was necessary to carry on what had once been begun so as to bring it to completion, at least in that degree in which it was then possible to do so, in order that in future it might attain its full stature.

Thus it was possible for the Conference to take place in London, and a large number of persons from the continent of Europe and the English-speaking peoples, both members and non-members, took part in it. The address of welcome written by Herr Albert Steffen, who owing to pressure of work was unfortunately unable to be present in person, was very warmly received. Several representatives of different countries followed with opening addresses. I am not here concerned so much with giving a detailed account of what was said but rather with giving a general picture of the whole atmosphere.

The first two days ran their course extremely well, albeit with a somewhat exclusive attendance, but from then onwards the public became more and more interested.

The lectures and demonstrations were representative of the whole range of Anthroposophy and its manifold practical results, and these appealed in ever-increasing degree to the general public, and also aroused the interest of the Press, so that many notices and pictures appeared in the newspapers.

So it has been possible to carry the message of the fruitfulness of Anthroposophy into wider circles. The name and work of Rudolf Steiner have found their way into this city of millions, and an opportunity was given not only to those who had perhaps already come into touch with Anthroposophy to be brought nearer to it but also to awaken the attention of others who had never heard of it before. Between the lectures, many of our friends had the opportunity of speaking to such people, and these described how much it had meant to them to come into contact with Anthroposophy and how they intended to interest themselves in it still further. To many it was the art that had been inaugurated by Rudolf Steiner which primarily appealed to them, to others perhaps the science, and to others again the religion.

Dr Steiner's educational work, which has hitherto had its activities principally on the Continent, is gaining more and more ground in England, and was well represented in the lectures and exhibitions. One continental Board of Education had commissioned a certain person, who was present at the

Conference, to examine how far Rudolf Steiner's pedagogy had taken root in England.

The Dornach eurythmy demonstrated to crowded and highly-delighted audiences what a rich gift it has to bring to mankind.

The various lectures on the medical work, given by several doctors who were present, revealed what are its fundamental principles and aims. And demonstrations of curative eurythmy, with an explanatory address, and accompanied by music composed by Edmund Pracht and played on the instruments specially designed by Lothar Gärtner, gave a picture of the effectiveness of our art of movement when it is applied to healing purposes.

This art of movement is also an integral part of curative education. An exhibition of paintings, carvings and modellings done by children gave further evidence of how rich a blessing this curative education can be for children who are defective or backward in soul or body. The exhibits also gave an excellent example of the different stages of the curative process.

There are great possibilities for the furtherance of this work in England where so much is being done in the social sphere.

In future a great deal will be able to be accomplished with music as a part of this curative education. The first beginnings have already been made, not only in the form of the new musical instruments, which appeal so much more to the souls of the children than the 'dead' piano, but also in the selection of the musical 'modes' to suit the particular stage of the child's development, and further by practising a kind of curative singing. This has been worked out, and tested for many years, by Frau Werbeck of Hamburg, on suggestions and advice given to her by Dr Steiner. This is the first time it has been made public.

In this way the many-sided activities of the medical work were well represented. And furthermore, they were consolidated by the scientific work of Frau Kolisko and Herr Ehrenfried Pfeiffer. All that had been said medically with regard to the influences of the cosmos upon man, animal and plant could be deepened by the proofs given in their lectures of the activity of the stars upon plants and earthly substances. And so theory and practice were united together, and the audiences were greatly interested.

Much could be said about the many other beautiful lectures, only this would take us too far. But I should like to mention Mrs Merry's opening lecture, and the words she spoke at the end of the Conference, which were given as the answer from a western soul to the souls of Middle Europe; also the warm concluding address given by Mr Dunlop. Each day had its own distinctive colouring, and was rich in variety, since Anthroposophy in word and Anthroposophy in deed were there in fullness, and could give a beautiful impression of Rudolf Steiner's work.

It is a matter for the deepest satisfaction that such a Conference could be organized precisely in the West. For the West is the guardian of human civilization, and it will only be able to fulfil its task if it can transplant anthroposophical impulses which are nurtured at the Goetheanum, ever more and more into the processes of life.

The Conference was attended—so I was informed by someone responsible for the exits and entrances—by non-members of the Society numbering about 2,000 persons all told. Some of the lectures had audiences of about 800. Frau Werbeck's concert, which took place towards the close, and which was a most artistic event, quite filled the hall. And although a good many people had already left, those who remained till the very last day could return to their homes fully satisfied with everything.

On Rudolf Steiner

An address given to commemorate his birthday,
27 February 1931
in Rudolf Steiner Hall, London

My dear friends,

Today, on 27 February, it is appropriate for us to direct our
thoughts even more than we otherwise do to Rudolf Steiner,
to concern ourselves in thought with him, to bring to life our
memories of his person, his gestures, his deeds. And if I may
speak to you here about this wonderful man, you must forgive
me if out of his extensive life I wish to place in the foreground
chiefly what happened in the last years and what I was
especially privileged to experience.

You will have read in his autobiography how Rudolf Steiner
spent his youth and the time of his later work, and how his
development culminated in vision of the supersensible
worlds. 'The visionary consciousness' is what he called this
seership. With this vision into the supersensible world he
proclaimed a spiritual science that has as content the teaching
of the Gods, the teaching of the true human being and his
relationship to Earth and Heaven, and the teaching of the
cosmos.

I should like in passing to mention here a matter of
exceptional value for the assessment of Rudolf Steiner's
personality. With this type of seership there had come something quite new, which was not there before in any human
being. In earlier times it had certainly been possible to receive
tidings from the spiritual world, but this always happened
half-consciously or in a mediumistic way. To receive such
tidings in the conscious manner in which Rudolf Steiner

received them was a phenomenon with which all occultists of the present time were preoccupied, because in their opinion one could not attain any other consciousness than that which could reach as far as the Moon sphere. Their opinion was that it was not possible to know anything beyond the secrets of the Moon, and so for those who were in the know in occult societies it was a riddle that one could speak about secrets of the Sun, secrets of the planets, and about the evolution of the Earth in relation to the whole cosmos in the way that Rudolf Steiner did.

The Christ-Being as a cosmic being was brought into clear daylight and thereby the relationship of the Christ to the Sun and the Earth was made known. Shattering secrets about the relation of Christ to the human soul were not only told to a collection of people who had grouped themselves around him and later formed themselves into the Anthroposophical Society; they were also made known to everybody who wanted to hear them.

This brought about a hostility, an opposition against Rudolf Steiner, coming from people who, as he expressed it, had antiquated ideas about the relationships of the sensible and supersensible worlds. Thus within the Theosophical Society opposition arose from its leading personalities, who did not want to accept Rudolf Steiner's knowledge, his 'Sun-knowledge', and showed no inclination to come to grips with his conscious seership. Other opposition arose from occult societies, who everywhere brought out their human instruments in the form of opponents combating Rudolf Steiner's teachings.

And Rudolf Steiner names very precisely the time when the opposition against him came out into the open: it was when he had brought to conclusion his cycle *From Jesus to Christ*.

Despite all animosity Rudolf Steiner went calmly on his way. He went all through the spiritual world just as exactly as a geologist goes over the Earth, and brought his findings down in such a way that they could be grasped by present-day thinking. That was what was exceptionally interesting in Rudolf Steiner. Unnoticed by the people confronting him, he transformed scientific thinking into imaginative thinking, and this was again grasped by day-consciousness; and he transposed what was imagined into concepts and mental pictures. So it was always a continuous transformation of day-consciousness into seership and vice versa.

I often heard him say about himself that the Imaginations were really always there, and day-consciousness only had to intervene so that they could be regulated and put in order. 'Yes,' he once said, 'I am on Earth and in Heaven at the same time, and while I look at you I experience you, and your supersensible being tells me significant things. I know what is around you.' And it was often the case that after a meeting or a talk Rudolf Steiner would suddenly take paper and pencil and draw a picture, perhaps of a face, or a landscape, a picture of columns, or scenery deriving from ancient times and connected with him or with me or with other people. It often happened that I would ask this or that and the answer would then come in a wonderful lecture. Many people have had similar experiences of having the answer to their questions given in a lecture.

I would here like to go more into this secret of asking a question. Important things, very significant things, were said by Rudolf Steiner if at a particular moment the right question was asked. 'A karma could be resolved through a particular question,' he would say.

And with that I would like to tell how one day I was standing in front of him and asked, 'What I am seeking is a form of medicine based upon the mysteries; could the doctors inside the Society receive this?' He answered in the affirmative, and that was the beginning of my medical work with Rudolf Steiner, the first impulse for the founding of the Medical Section.

In the same way Emil Molt asked him whether he would be willing to take on the direction of a school, that Molt had founded for the children of the Waldorf cigarette factory. Rudolf Steiner agreed, and Waldorf education came into being.

Curative education came about by three people asking him for advice as to how retarded children should be treated. And one could give many other examples. It always depended on things being linked to individual persons, who then also had to bear full responsibility for further progress and development.

There were always many people coming to Rudolf Steiner to ask him for advice. And here one could make a very striking observation. He always gave his advice in such a way that one followed it readily and willingly, as if he knew quite well that the advice should be given in this way and no other. It was not given from the standpoint of the person giving it but from the standpoint of the person requesting it, and also with an eye to the questioner's ability to accept it. Rudolf Steiner read in one's soul what one wanted, and he bestowed his advice accordingly. Why? So as to preclude apparently unpleasant advice from not being taken up. Many people do not want to follow unpleasant advice, and failure to follow advice given by Rudolf Steiner would have karmic consequences. Rudolf Steiner wanted to protect the person in question from these karmic consequences, to guard him from the possibility of coming into opposition with him. He could think in this way because he had a high mission. This adaptation to the person, to the individual's stage of development, was an outstanding feature in his dealings with people. It might happen that he would sternly demand something from those who were in a position to act as he had advised, or might give patient and loving advice. It is therefore impossible properly to assess something said by Rudolf Steiner if it is separated from the person to whom he said it.

For this reason it was often said to be difficult always to understand Rudolf Steiner in his dealings with people, in the directions he would give. What I have said here should explain much in this connection. With Rudolf Steiner everything was immersed in a never-failing human love. There was endless compassion in his soul for the pain and blindness of mankind, and no sacrifice or trouble was too great for him in helping to remove the veil from men's eyes. And the work on humanity's behalf that Rudolf Steiner achieved in the last two years of his life is almost inconceivable. Through the burning of the Goetheanum, which left his physical body a wreck, there took place a severe loosening of his ether body and a partial separation of his ether body from his physical body—

his health became more and more delicate. 'Compared with other men I am actually already dead on the Earth,' he would often say, 'my ego and astral body direct the physical body and supplement the ethereal.'

Yes, my dear friends, one could just tremble when hearing such a saying, and it seemed like a gift of divine grace that Rudolf Steiner was still here.

One could experience that he took it himself to be a gift of grace from the way in which he tirelessly set to work to awaken the Society from the lethargy into which it had fallen, and to give it new impulses. During the time between the fire and the refounding of the Society, there was a constant struggle to find ways and possibilities to urge the members to more intensive work. He always called this the galvanizing of the Society. 'The Society as it is run cannot develop further unless it is newly enlivened,' he would often say. I had the good fortune to participate in this time intensively. It was shattering to see the disappointments in human beings that Rudolf Steiner then experienced. People did not understand what he wanted, people did not want to take up new impulses, so that it even came to such a pass that he considered abandoning the Anthroposophical Society and working somewhere with a small group of people chosen by himself. At the very last hour—it was the end of November 1923—he then resolved to exert all his energies in taking on himself the leadership of the Anthroposophical Society, not just as teacher and adviser but as real leader in the sense that nothing could happen without his initiative and will.

This resolve could be seen coming to effect like a tremendous will-impulse in the lectures on the mysteries, which shortly afterwards were then bestowed on us. Then everything went further in quick succession: the Christmas Foundation Meeting was given, in which he founded the Society anew, and took its leadership on himself with his own appointed *Vorstand*. This was seemingly taken up with great enthusiasm. But was it really taken up in the hearts of men? The invocation of the elemental beings, called up to bear witness in the laying of the Foundation Stone, and the plea for human beings to hear it did not achieve what they should have achieved.

Human ears remained deaf, and the elemental beings waited in expectation of what might come from men and became restless when insufficient echo came back from them, Dr Steiner said. Then he spoke about a promise which he had given to the spiritual world and had to keep if things did not change.

What kind of promise was it which he had to keep? He never spoke it out, but it seemed to me as if the offering that he had brought for us in uniting the Anthroposophical Movement, which he embodied, with the Anthroposophical Society had to be better understood, and he could only stay with us if more understanding were to arise for the ideas of the Christmas Foundation Meeting. And when that seemed not to be the case, he left us. Many remarks by Rudolf Steiner to the effect that among the members there was still not much understanding for the Christmas Foundation Meeting confirmed this for me. I will not speak further about these things here as they could also be misinterpreted, but I must mention that personally I suffer beyond words when I remember that I might not have done all I could to understand the Christmas Foundation Meeting. And the responsibility that weighs on one, not to have experienced Rudolf Steiner's last year as wakefully as one might have wished, while one was around him hourly every day, this responsibility is unspeakably heavy to bear. I will here pass over the painful hours, weeks and months when he lay on his sick-bed, which was in the Studio of the Carpentry-shop and was under my supervision. It is really not possible to describe the battles that were waged in those still hours against the onslaught of inimical powers. (And if I add the picture that so often appeared to me, the picture of Catholic priests with evil wishes, then you can imagine how much suffering there was at this sick-bed.)

But in spite of everything, there was in Rudolf Steiner endless patience, love and desire to work. His sublime spirit came down so as to be in a physical body for 25 years as a leader of mankind on Earth, and so as to be now a teacher of dead human beings and other spiritual beings in the super-sensible world. There too they need him.

Here I would like to try and answer a question which is

continually raised: what is to be understood by the illness of an initiate? Why was it said that Rudolf Steiner was ill?

Well, why did he become ill? His delicate physical body was abandoned too much and too long by his soul and spirit, which were working in their very own domain. His physical body was given over to its own heaviness and physical laws, so that it became weaker and nourishment stopped working. Nonetheless there could have been an improvement if destiny, if his own sublime being, had willed it, and if it had been necessary for the karma of the world.

I am firmly convinced that Rudolf Steiner would have become better had it not been needful to cut short his earthly life and take over the direction of world events from another plane. For even during his illness he still made very many plans, for instance, to undertake a journey to Palestine and Greece as soon as he was recovered. As another instance, he also had the neighbouring room set up so that he could start to model and paint the interior decoration of the Goetheanum. These were surely things which gave one hope that his health would recover. But one day he said that everything would take a different course, that I had to have very great courage, and that worlds would totter if I did not have the courage to carry out what the future demanded of me. He had not been completely followed, he said, sadly but still lovingly, like someone who had forgiven and had already turned his thoughts to other and greater life tasks. This was the turning point, as if a heavenly council had taken place which had decided the future, binding on Rudolf Steiner, binding on those people who have united themselves to Rudolf Steiner.

Binding on Rudolf Steiner, who wished to keep his promise to the spiritual world.

Binding on the members, who had to choose, completely out of freedom, whether they wished to remain true to him beyond death.

In many people there lives the burning question: is Rudolf Steiner still united with us after his death? If we did not understand him during his life, is it possible to understand him now, and will he remain the leader of men on Earth who declare themselves for him, even though he is not incarnated in a physical body? My dear friends, after death only reality has any effect. If feelings expressing reverence and true love rise up to him and a reunion with him takes place out of freedom, then he will stay real for us and remain our leader beyond death and life.

The strange opinion that after the death of Rudolf Steiner one does not feel him really working among us any more can only be held by someone having no feeling of being united with him.

If one has this feeling of being united with him, as one has with a beloved human being, then one feels the presence of Rudolf Steiner everywhere and no power on Earth will be able to sever one from him. One feels his help, his love, in everything that one does, even if one's actions are not free from mistakes.

What must be understood at the present time is the courageous activity which is demanded of one in the Michaelic Age, so that one may help in the re-forming of earthly conditions. Michael is not to be found in contemplative tranquillity but in the battle against traditional concepts and ideas which are no longer suitable in our present-day civilization. And so we will end with the verse Rudolf Steiner gave to those whom he described as belonging to Michael.*

* Translator's note: The allusion is to the verse given by Rudolf Steiner at the end of his 'last address'. On the present occasion this was followed by a speech-choir recital of verses from I Corinthians 13.

On Rudolf Steiner

An address given to commemorate his birthday,
27 February 1933
in Rudolf Steiner Hall, London

Dear Friends,

Though for the past eight years Rudolf Steiner has no longer
been among us in the physical body, one cannot feel that he
has departed from us. And in these difficult times we are
reminded of many a word he spoke and of many a situation.
For in the long run all things are connected with one another.
Every one of us who knew Rudolf Steiner will be able to recall
things he said on one or other occasion, and we can thus
throw light on many things that now appear dark to us.
Inevitably in these recollections things of a more personal
character will occur, for we relate the experiences that we
ourselves had with Rudolf Steiner. But we can only obtain a
fuller picture of Rudolf Steiner if each of us tells what he
himself can recall and in this way (many)* people (who did
not know him) can learn to understand how he was united
with all, how he was there indeed for all mankind. This alone
is the purpose of the reminiscences I shall now relate.

It was on a beautiful summer's day that as a young medical
student I visited Rudolf Steiner at Friedrichshagen near
Berlin. He had just become General Secretary of the German
Section of the Theosophical Society. I had no other purpose
than to enquire about the theosophical work and to obtain a
direct impression of Rudolf Steiner, of whom it was said in

* Translator's note: Material in brackets is taken from a hitherto unpublished typescript; see p. 14.

Dutch theosophical circles that in esoteric matters he had paths of his own, differing from those of Annie Besant, who at that time was held in high esteem in those circles. It was also said that he was too German, that in his lectures he dealt over much with German philosophers, which was something new and unaccustomed in the theosophical movement, for the latter was more inclined to turn in the direction of oriental teachings.

Rudolf Steiner asked me what I was doing in Berlin. 'Studying,' I answered, 'and learning to know life.' He looked at me searchingly and, without saying anything more, handed me a syllabus of his forthcoming lectures, as though he would give a certain direction to the 'learning to know life'. We understood one another very well. I promised to come to his lectures and took my departure. I wondered at the syllabus. There were lectures on German literature (and no Theosophy, I thought, for) the word 'Theosophy' did not occur at all. Dr Steiner was indeed going along paths of his own. For some he was too German, for others not German enough. In his lecture syllabuses he used or did not use the word 'Theosophy' according to what his purpose was at the time. The Theosophical Society, such as it was then, did not like it.

I did not go to many of his lectures, but one (that I heard in the Architektenhaus in Berlin) interested me especially. It was on Goethe's *Fairy Tale of the Green Snake and the Beautiful Lily*. After the lecture I asked Rudolf Steiner if it was not possible to learn more about esoteric truths. He replied briefly and significantly, 'Come to Motzstrasse 17,' naming the day and hour. I appeared on the appointed day and took part in an esoteric lesson. From that moment onward I knew that Rudolf Steiner was and is my teacher, and will be so in the future. As to Theosophy as taught in Holland through Annie Besant—I found my way to it while still in Holland—I now felt it childish compared with what Rudolf Steiner gave. Many, many people have been helped in this way by gaining insight into esoteric teachings through Rudolf Steiner. By the sudden impulse into their inner life they were led once more to find themselves. The riddle of existence received a new meaning. One knew that one had a place and a specific task to fulfil in life.

The keen and active work in Berlin and throughout Germany, the marvellous lectures which Rudolf Steiner gave in many towns and cities of that country, laid the foundations of the spiritual movement which took its start from him and which has now become known throughout the world under the name of Anthroposophy.

Rudolf Steiner had never yet been to Switzerland and the time was now approaching when this was destined to come about. Human beings had to be there to help him in this direction, and my destiny led me to this task. Having attended the frequent lectures and lecture courses in Berlin for a time, I went to Switzerland to continue my medical studies. (There were not yet many people there interested in Rudolf Steiner's work.) There were only two members of the Theosophical Society living in Zurich at that time. (With these two old members) I was now able to arrange a lecture for Dr Steiner there, and he entered Switzerland shortly afterwards. I mention this because his arrival there was of great significance for the further development of Anthroposophy. It was the beginning of a series of important visits to Zurich, Basle and Berne, and found its culmination or I should rather say its new beginning in the erection of the Goetheanum on the Dornach hill in the year 1914.

Dr Steiner gave the whole esoteric Christology in Switzerland. He proclaimed the deeper meaning of the four Gospels and spoke of the relations of the Iro-Scottish monks who were the bearers of an esoteric Christianity to St Gallen, the historic town in northern Switzerland. Many things of deep esoteric significance were given out in Switzerland, so much so that one might regard it as a preparation for what afterwards went out from Dornach and the Goetheanum.

(It would lead too far if I were to mention every talk, every important encounter with Rudolf Steiner. He was interested in everything, and) I should here like to tell of a visit of his to Villa Wesendonck in the neighbourhood of Zurich. Richard Wagner, as you are probably aware, was on terms of friendship with Frau Mathilde Wesendonck and lived for a time in the small country house adjoining the villa (where he composed the beginning of *Parsifal*).

Now in those times it was not Rudolf Steiner's custom to drive to places comfortably in a motor car. He liked (had time then) to take long walks in order to get the impression of the whole neighbourhood. His way of doing it made a deep impression on me. It was the surrounding country that in this case chiefly interested Rudolf Steiner—the view of the Zurich lake, the hills and so on. In all humility I would like to say it seemed to me as though he wanted to test the spirituality of the whole atmosphere—to see how much spirituality was still there and of what kind. He then expressed himself to the effect that the matter-of-fact simplicity (but at the same time also the purity) of the surroundings had had as it were an effect of suction on the great fulness of Wagner's life and had drawn forth what lay slumbering deep down in his soul.

Rudolf Steiner was greatly interested in Richard Wagner. He always emphasized the world-embracing character of Wagner's creations, and his significance for all mankind. Nowadays, when so much is nationalistic, it is wonderfully refreshing to recall how Rudolf Steiner always revealed the supra-national character of the great spirits of mankind. They were universal, and there for all men.

I felt the Munich Congress especially as of immense significance. In the year 1907 a great Theosophical Congress was held in Munich; all the important theosophists from all countries were congregated there. Annie Besant, too, was present. (Rudolf Steiner went on other ways than Leadbeater and Annie Besant, and there was great excitement among her friends.) One could well observe how the question constantly went round in their circle as to whence Rudolf Steiner derived his immense knowledge of the spiritual world. They themselves had no such knowledge and they knew of no one from whom they might receive it. And when Rudolf Steiner himself stated to Annie Besant that his knowledge extended not only to the Moon sphere, as in the case of ancient oriental wisdom, but that in waking condition he could reach with his consciousness as far as the Sun sphere, because he spoke in this way, he was regarded as heretical, proud and presumptuous. Through my connections with Annie Besant's Dutch friends I had an opportunity to observe the keen interest with which the case of Rudolf Steiner was discussed. The *new* thing that had made its appearance, namely, that an occultist could reach up as far as the Sun sphere with his consciousness, the old esoteric circles could not understand.

Very soon afterwards Dr Steiner sent for me. I knew that a decisive moment of my life was approaching, and that I had to decide either to follow Rudolf Steiner completely and entirely and to make known to him this decision, or to remain instead (with the Dutch friends) on the old path.

Rudolf Steiner received me earnestly, with a questioning look. (Not many words passed between us, we understood one another very well.) Feeling that he was expecting something from me, I said quite simply: 'I will stay with you.'

His look became radiant, he took my hand, gave me the Sign of Michael, and told me important things that I may not repeat. (A karmic relationship that he and I had developed in very ancient times was now renewed between us.)

Only after many years did I become conscious of the import of this moment. (Just as, later on, Rudolf Steiner's work so shaped itself as then to lead in 1923 to the laying of the Foundation Stone of the new Anthroposophical Society, so did this meeting then play a part in making it possible for Rudolf Steiner to begin the medical work with me within the Anthroposophical Movement. But before this could happen I needed to let all this sink deeply into me and quietly carry through my studies to the end.) It was on the occasion of the laying of the Foundation Stone of the Anthroposophical Society in 1923 when I was given the leadership of the Medical Section and when the First Class was founded. I was filled with a deep sense of responsibility, to remain true through all difficulties to Rudolf Steiner and to continue faithful throughout the time to come.

I would now like to try to awaken understanding for the way in which Rudolf Steiner built up his work and for the impulses he followed. For this we shall need to call up in memory the history of the evolution of mankind with its great epochs of culture.

Three thousand years before Christ, mankind began to

acquire a new condition of consciousness. An older humanity had the ego still outside the body; the ego still hovered around the body. Hence this older humanity was more nearly united with the spiritual world. Abraham was the first human being organically so constituted that the ego could take possession of him. As this came about, he and his descendants gradually lost the faculty of seeing into the spiritual world. The spiritual world became closed to them. Therefore this era has been named Kali Yuga, the Dark Age, and the first thousand years of it was called the Age of Abraham.

Two thousand years before Christ was the Age of Moses. In this Age, the Deity worked from without. He made Himself known to man externally, for example by means of thunder and lightning, as was the case with Moses. Men were guided by means of outer commandments because they needed such outer guidance.

From the period 1000 to 900 BC we have the beginning of the Age of Solomon. The knowledge of man was pursued during this Age. The Temple was built which King Solomon saw spiritually but could not bring to realization on Earth without the help of the architect Hiram Abiff. The Temple was a symbol of the physical body. In the Temple there had to be the brazen sea as a symbol of the right working together of ether body, astral body and ego.

It was known that there were two kinds of generations of men upon Earth: the generation that sprang from the priesthood or the priest kings, of whom King Solomon was a representative, and the generation of the sons of Cain, of whom Hiram Abiff was a representative. These latter had acquired a knowledge of the Earth. They knew how to deal with measure, number and weight, and they knew how to give form and shape to matter—they had the right knowledge for dealing with things of Earth. The representatives of the Solomon generation received wisdom direct from the spiritual world but were not able with this knowledge to bring anything to realization upon Earth—the knowledge remained a theory. The friendship of Solomon with Hiram opened the way for something new. It became possible for the spiritual men to stand firmly on the Earth, as symbolized in the

Temple, the brazen sea, the hammer and the sacred Tau sign, which is connected with the ego, and the sacred triangle, the symbol of Manas, Buddhi, Atma.

While the generation of Solomon had the wisdom that rests within itself, the generation of Cain had the wisdom that was united with the astral fire. In order that he might gain control over the astral fire, Hiram received through an initiation the power to use the Tau sign, whereby the ego could become lord over the passions and desires.

The myth relates how this initiation of Hiram took place while he was engaged in the casting of the brazen sea. He could not succeed with the casting; instead of becoming brass it became liquid, and fire broke out of it. This happened because a conflict had broken out between Solomon and Hiram, a conflict in which soul qualities such as doubt, personal feelings and superstition played a part. This prevented the casting from taking place smoothly and harmoniously, and Hiram was called upon to throw himself into the fire. The meaning is that in that moment he was initiated. He received the Tau sign, the triangle and the knowledge of the Word. When he came to himself again he was able to restore the brazen sea and make it right.

The conflict between Solomon and Hiram was, however, not yet ended, not even when Hiram was killed. The two generations of men could not live together in harmony. Both were fighting for the soul, symbolized in the Queen of Sheba—the soul who had complete and universal understanding. Solomon wanted, through union with this soul, to attain to the fullness of manhood. Hiram, on the other hand, through the freely offered gifts of this soul, wished to be removed to higher spheres.

It was in this Age that the Mystery of Golgotha took place. Christ Jesus was the first who was able to bridge the gulf between the two. By the initiation of Lazarus—who bore in him the reincarnated individuality of Hiram—to be the disciple John, Christ Jesus was able to bridge over the Mystery of Solomon and Hiram. The son of Cain, Hiram–Lazarus–John, was initiated through Christ Himself. In John was concentrated the whole of esoteric knowledge, and moreover that also which was connected with John the Baptist as esoteric Christianity. It is the being of Christian Rosenkreuz who is the bearer of the knowledge throughout this subsequent time. (All secrets of the being of man are with the Rosicrucians, all true Christology.)

The Age of Solomon continues still after Christ for a thousand years in a Christianized form. And then comes a repetition of the Age of Moses, also in a new form. No longer is the divine sought ouside man, but within. The divine made itself known within the souls of the mystics; and Johannes Tauler could say that the divine within him worked through his words like thunder and lightning upon his hearers, and the man who has Christ within him has the outer law in his heart. So that one may speak of a Christianized Age of Moses.

And now we are once again in a new Age of Abraham. Since the ego united itself for the first time (in Abraham) with the physical body, it has been able to be active for thousands of years, and it has at length brought man to self-consciousness, purified the soul and guided it to higher functions. Now the time has come when the ego is to set itself free again from the bodily and concern itself with the unfolding of the higher members of man's being. It is into this new Age of Abraham that the activity of Rudolf Steiner is placed.

And now Rudolf Steiner proceeded to build up his Anthroposophy in the following manner.

First of all he gave a groundwork (in his esoteric teaching) with the wisdom of Solomon and Hiram, the wisdom of the macrocosm and the microcosm, giving it in such a way that those endowed with the power of the ego were able to receive it.

After that came the knowledge of the Christ-Being as a Cosmic Being and as the Christ in us. From Moses to Johannes Tauler; from the period of the Christ–Yahveh activity to the period of the Christ–Jesus activity—and all the time, streaming in like a ray of light, the ego-power, which belongs essentially to the Abraham Age.

(Through this the principle of freedom must now also come.) Hence we find as preparation for Rudolf Steiner's work the book *Philosophy of Freedom*, where the man who is strong in his ego is called upon to set the ego free again for higher stages of evolution. (Human beings must be brought to freedom and insight, and in freedom they must take their development in hand—not doing what is right because of an outer law but because the voice of conscience speaks inside. Rudolf Steiner wanted to bring mankind to this development.)

Then Rudolf Steiner wanted to show in his work how the right understanding for the Christ could come (only by way of Greece) through the Greek philosophy, which was steeped in mystery wisdom. (The preparation for this understanding was cultivated in the various mystery centres in Asia Minor and Greece.) And here is the line that is connected with Rudolf Steiner's own individuality. In Ephesus the Mysteries of the Word were guarded and cultivated, that is, the understanding was awakened for the descent of the Christ to Earth. It was Yahveh through whom the Christ expressed Himself, Yahveh Elohim who as Moon God brought about the condition of balance between Sun, Moon and Earth. Michael was his messenger.

It was within the time when Michael as Archangel had the leadership of the Greek epoch that the Ephesian Mysteries came to their full flower of development and became known far and wide through all lands. Ephesus was in those days the centre of all cultures. And it was the philosopher Cratylus who was deeply united with these Mysteries and was able to bring them to life in the heart of Plato.

Through Plato, Ephesus found a continuation in Eleusis. In the Eleusinian Mysteries it is now no longer the descent of the divine which men hear about but the suffering that the divine soul, who wanders upon Earth, has to undergo. There were taught the secrets of the birth, evolution and ascent of the soul. The life of the Earth was spoken of in its connection with Sun and Moon, as well as Christ-dedicated divine beings experiencing their destinies, such as Persephone and Demeter.

It devolved upon Aristotle to drive back these mysteries with his philosophy and to lead men further in thought. In reality this could only come about after a sufficient number of souls had received the mysteries with deep inwardness while on Earth and were thus able to continue to live with them even beyond death. The possibility was thereby created for these teachings to come alive again in later times.

(The content of these mysteries was given once more in the spiritual world in a spiritual school that was led by Michael. And these people, who, in the spiritual world, had followed Michael's call, and those who are deeply bound up with esoteric Christianity, who follow the direction of Lazarus–John and have had Michael as Night Spirit to inspire them, must always go together, should mankind come into the right evolution.) Michael, who had advanced from being a servant of Christ–Yahveh to being a servant of Christ, and who was closely bound up with the wisdom of Christian Rosenkreuz as well as with the Greek Mysteries, will now draw all these together in the spiritual world through his Michael School, and on Earth through the fact that he has become the Time Spirit of our civilization. Rudolf Steiner gave us this knowledge.

The guidance of man is not yet at an end. Still hidden from us is the great spirit who as Mani will lead mankind on further. Mightily will this individuality intervene in the guidance of mankind. To indulge in speculation about this individuality is unworthy. We must await in truth and humility what is revealed to us.

I would like to end here with an expression of my unbounded trust in the guidance of Michael and in the help of Rudolf Steiner, and of my hope that more and more people may continually be awakened to understand how great a step forward Rudolf Steiner has brought mankind with his teaching, and with his example of how to live on Earth.

Dr Ita Wegman
by George Adams

April-May 1943

Dr Ita Wegman died at Arlesheim, Switzerland, on Thursday 4 March 1943—according to the telegrams we received, at 9.55 in the morning. Of the Executive or *Vorstand* chosen by Rudolf Steiner to work with him when the Anthroposophical Society was founded under his presidency at Christmas, 1923, she is the first to follow him into the spiritual world—nearly 18 years after his passing.

Born in the Dutch East Indies in 1876, Dr Wegman at her death was 67 years old. As a young medical student, studying in Germany and Switzerland, she had joined the Society, i.e. the Section of the Theosophical Society of which Dr Steiner was General Secretary, very soon after its inception in the year 1902. She was well known to Rudolf Steiner throughout those years and became an active member of the Zurich Group. After the War, when the medical and other practical branches of spiritual work were growing, she came to Arlesheim and founded the Clinical-Therapeutic Institute. During the last year or two before the Christmas Foundation Meeting of 1923, it became ever more evident that Rudolf Steiner recognized in her his chosen collaborator for the development of anthroposophical medicine: a collaboration which then found expression in the joint authorship of a fundamental text-book.

In the tragic time of the Goetheanum fire and the year 1923, Dr Wegman took an active part in rousing the Anthroposophical Society to a fuller consciousness of its tasks and opportunities. At the Foundation itself, Rudolf Steiner appointed her to the position of Recorder in the *Vorstand* of the Society, while at the same time she became leader of the Medical Section in the School of Spiritual Science. As

Recorder, Dr Wegman worked at Dr Steiner's side and bore important responsibilities, especially in the more esoteric work which was then initiated. It was clear from Rudolf Steiner's words that his collaboration with her at this time was based on very deep foundations and was a deep spiritual help to him. In lectures of the year 1924 we ourselves heard him refer to her as his collaborator not only in the field of medicine but in the wider field of spiritual science as a whole. In the Torquay lectures he dwelt on this in an even more specific way. We may perhaps mention one respect in which it was quite evident that Dr Wegman helped him. During the years of intense and many-sided work after the War, when so many fields of work were initiated by him and many active and enthusiastic workers were constantly taking counsel with him, trying their best to work under his leadership, Rudolf Steiner suffered deeply from the intellectual hardness of the time, a quality of which very, very few of us were free. In Dr Wegman, with all her ability and energy, he found another quality of intelligence—less clever, perhaps, less gifted in outward forms of expression, but more gentle, more perceptive, more in contact with the universe around her. This was something more than rest and solace to him.

In looking back upon the life that is now ended, it is perhaps good that we recall this characteristic of Dr Ita Wegman, which was so often a stone of offence to us who lacked it. The world's present sorrows, the full bitterness of which we have not nearly tasted, are due to the want of that new kind of intelligence—or to the fact that men are still relying so entirely upon the old and do not seek the new, even where it is near at hand. In the last years of his life, Rudolf Steiner was giving expression to certain impulses which from the inmost heart of the Time-Spirit could bring salvation to Europe and the modern world. They were the impulses connected first with the Threefold Order in social life; then with the perception of threefold man (head, heart and limbs) with all that it implied for medicine, education and the sciences and arts; last but not least, with the Christmas Foundation Meeting. To live and create out of these perceptions calls for that new way of thinking in which Dr Wegman was far ahead of the great majority, and in respect of which—so far as her active life was concerned—Rudolf Steiner's passing left her very lonely.

In the winter of 1924/5 Dr Wegman nursed and tended Rudolf Steiner through the long months of his illness and scarcely left his side. The experience of these few years—from the Goetheanum fire until Rudolf Steiner's passing—left an indelible impression on her. After his death she remained filled with the great impulses of the Christmas Foundation Meeting—impulses, hopes, also anxieties on behalf of mankind, which he had shared with her in many an intimate conversation. These impulses, connected as they were with the more world-wide active character which the Anthroposophical Movement was now to take, inspired her through and through, and all the sorrow and solemnity connected with Rudolf Steiner's passing was in her way of life received into this atmosphere. What he had said of the co-operation between earthly and spiritual worlds was so real to her that in her writing and speaking at that time (as we may read again in *Anthroposophical Movement*, the weekly news-sheet of the Goetheanum, for the year 1925), she tended to emphasize rather the continuity of the work and purpose of *Michaelites* both here and yonder than the sudden and irreparable loss which for a more earthly piety—also true and necessary in its way—was the overwhelming outcome of our teacher's death.

Dr Wegman never could reconcile herself to the fact that this attitude was unacceptable, as indeed it proved to be to a large and in time ever more influential section, notably among the older members. That the motives of it were misunderstood was a source of untold suffering for her. The thing outstanding in Dr Wegman was love of the great impulses of spiritual regeneration of humanity *in the way of Michael*, and her relation to all fellow-anthroposophists without exception was steeped in this enthusiasm. In consequence of this—as it was also of her natural cordiality, her imaginative, generous and ever-buoyant interest in all her fellow-men—she could quickly forget and forgive all offences and misunderstandings, take blame upon herself, and renew fellowship if only the way was opened out in active pursuit of the great impulses which in her heart she always saw and lived with. I know of no better way of characterizing Dr Wegman's forgivingness. It sprang from bounty.

An immense number of individuals were helped by Dr Wegman and many important activities were set on foot with her encouragement, often originally through her inspiration. Communities and institutions closely linked with her at their inception went their own independent way after a while. Not by a semblance of outward uniformity but by deeper and more living bonds she remained linked with them all. It is not unlikely that many people for a while became quite unconscious of the essential help they had received from her at one or another turning-point in their life; it would come back to them later.

Dr Wegman was very active in helping the movement in our country, as well as in her native Holland and in other and more distant lands. She had a close bond of co-operation—brought about, in fact, by Rudolf Steiner himself in his lifetime—with Mr Dunlop, continuing until the latter's death in 1935. During the time when we were still united with the Dornach centre, she tried again and again—as I myself can testify—to help us all to work together. In her advice she would counteract that exaggeration of wrongs and differences which comes about so easily when difficulties of a deeper kind arise in an occult movement. She did this freely and sincerely, because in fact—as I have indicated—she was humanly and deeply interested in all whom she contacted, even in those who might be wronging and misjudging her.

Not long before the eventual break came about—eight or nine years ago—Dr Wegman underwent a serious and prolonged illness. Although she fully recovered, from that time onwards the frustrations that had come to pass within the Society, and also, in the world at large, the ruthless tyrannies that were leading up to the present war, narrowed the scope of external work. During this time Dr Wegman, while continuing the medical work of the movement in the wide circle of her colleagues and disciples, turned with a great inner activity towards a deepened study and understanding of all Anthroposophy. Though I have only occasionally been present at the readings and study-circles which she conducted in these years, I have heard from many of the deep impressions they received. She entered now into the whole range of Rudolf Steiner's teaching, laying especial emphasis on all that was connected with the Christ-Impulse and the Mystery of Golgotha. There was in the way she did it the same inner fire, the same Michaelite enthusiasm with which she had once tried to inspire us, hoping for the fulfilment of the more outward and immediate tasks that had been bequeathed to us. Maybe in these later years she was very consciously preparing herself and others for what should be resumed in a future life.

At the General Meeting of our Society, in Rudolf Steiner House on 13 March, others who knew Dr Wegman better than I, or in other aspects of her life and work, spoke about her: Dr Stein, Dr König, Dr Mier, Mr Michael Wilson, Dr Heidenreich together created a picture whereby we could think of Dr Wegman with great love, recognizing anew how much she had helped others in their strivings. If I myself would sum up what I recall, with thankfulness and wonder, of Dr Wegman's being, I would refer to a passage in Rudolf Steiner's lectures on the Apocalypse of St John. It is where he speaks of Mercury as the Morning Star, and of the great change that comes to pass from the first to the second half of earthly planetary evolution.